Central Banking in
Theory and Practice

D0063072

The Lionel Robbins Lectures

Peter Temin, *Lessons from the Great Depression*, 1989

Paul R. Krugman, *Exchange-Rate Instability*, 1989

Jeffrey Sachs, *Poland's Jump to the Market Economy*, 1993

Pedro Aspe, *Economic Transformation the Mexican Way*, 1993

Yegor Gaidar and Karl Otto Pohl, *Russian Reform/International Money*, 1995

Robert J. Barro, *Determinants of Economic Growth: A Cross-Country Empirical Study*, 1997

Alan S. Blinder, *Central Banking in Theory and Practice*, 1998

Central Banking in
Theory and Practice

Alan S. Blinder

The MIT Press
Cambridge, Massachusetts
London, England

Midwood

Second MIT Press paperback edition, 1999

© 1998 Massachusetts Institute of Technology

This book was set in Palatino by Wellington Graphics and was printed and bound in the United States of America.

Library of Congress Cataloging-in-Publication Date

Blinder, Alan S.
  Central banking in theory and practice / Alan S. Blinder.
    p. cm. — (The Lionel Robbins lectures)
  Includes bibliographical references and index.
  ISBN 0-262-02439-X (hb: alk. paper), 0-262-52260-8 (pb)
  1. Banks and banking, Central. 2. Banks and banking, Central—United States. 3. Monetary policy. 4. Monetary policy—United States. I. Title. II. Series.
HG1811.B55 1998
332.1'1'0973—dc21   97-24961
                                                                      CIP

5/3/2000

To Shirley Blinder, with love.

Contents

Foreword

Central banks have never been more powerful than now. Monetary policy has become the central tool of macroeconomic stabilization, and in more and more countries monetary policy is in the hands of an independent central bank.

So how central banks operate really matters. To discuss this, there is no one better than Alan Blinder of Princeton University, who combines academic eminence with previous practical experience as Vice-Chairman of the Board of Governors of the Federal Reserve Board.

In these Lionel Robbins Memorial Lectures he argues powerfully that central banking can only be conducted effectively within a proper intellectual framework. This must be based on dynamic optimization, where each year we select a plan for now *and* for the future that will produce the best available time-path for output and inflation. This does not mean that policy becomes inflexible because the whole trick is to remake the plan each year. But unless we choose today's policy as part of a longer-term strategy, we shall tend to continue too long with a policy that is either too tight or too loose.

It was precisely this approach that led the Federal Reserve to tighten monetary policy in early 1994, knowing that they would probably loosen again in 1995. Only a process of hard thinking can lead to such choices, and there is always the danger that a committee will vote for more of the same, until there has been too much of it. Policy change must always be a lively option, though, as Brainard once pointed out, changes should always be smaller when uncertainty is present.

In his second lecture, Blinder moves to the concrete issues of the choice of monetary instrument and concludes that it must be the interest rate rather than any monetary aggregate. The reason is quite simply that money demand functions are impossibly unstable and that for most periods money is not even cointegrated with income. As Gerry Bouey, a former Governor of the Bank of Canada put it. "We didn't abandon the monetary aggregates, they abandoned us." Thus the IS curve rules, and the central bank must choose a path for short-term real interest rates in the context of what it believes to be the neutral real rate.

Thus Blinder dismisses old-style monetarism on the basis of Poole's original analysis of functional instabilities. He also dismisses the theory that time inconsistency will lead to excessive inflation, as argued by Barro and Gordon. This theory assumes that central banks would like to see output higher than the natural rate of output. But, as Blinder points out, this theory can neither explain why inflation rose from 1965–1980 nor why it fell from 1980–1995. Blinder attributes the rise from '65–'80 to supply shocks and claims that the subsequent fall shows that central banks will pursue low inflation and sustainable output without any artificial devices to overcome the problem of incentive compatibility.

Finally, Blinder addresses the question of whether the central bank should be independent and in what sense. He argues that it should be, since experience suggests that independent central banks deliver lower inflation without lower long-term growth.The reason for this superior performance is largely the lags between monetary policy actions and their results. A professional central bank with an ongoing existence has a greater incentive to deliver low inflation than a government which (whatever its declared objective) can get a quick output gain at the expense of higher ination later. A central bank has an incentive to develop its reputation for low inflation, so that even when it changes policy people do not believe it has changed its objectives. But Blinder rejects stronger versions of the credibility story according to which a credible central bank can change inflationary expectations in advance of lower actual inflation.

Is it undemocratic to have an independent central bank? Blinder thinks not. The goal of the bank should be set by politicians and its governors appointed by politicians (though with secure tenure). Independence means only operational freedom to control the instruments that affect the objectives. Moreover the bank should be open in its approach and give reasons for its actions. And this of course means that it has to have a clear intellectual framework that is well understood outside the bank as well as inside.

Professor Blinder's lectures show exactly how intellectual clarity can improve practical action. They should be read by policymakers worldwide. But only those who heard them could benefit from the fine manner of delivery, which matched the clarity of the argument. The trustees of the Lionel Robbins Memorial Fund are extremely grateful to Alan Blinder for this valuable contribution to a subject of such key importance.

Richard Layard
London School of Economics

Preface

I was not gone from the Federal Reserve Board very long when Richard Layard asked me to deliver the 1996 Robbins Lectures. The invitation presented me with an opportunity—and, more important, with a prod—to develop further some of the themes I had first enunciated in the Marshall Lectures at Cambridge in May 1995. Furthermore, since the Robbins Lectures were three rather than two, I could add substantial new material. And, as a private citizen rather than Vice Chairman of the Fed, I could speak my own mind freely with no fear that my words would be read as the official view of the Federal Reserve. I agreed with alacrity, and the book before you is the result.

While the manuscript leans toward the academic, I have tried to write it with two very different audiences in mind: on the one hand, teachers and students in universities and, on the other, real-world practitioners of the art of central banking (along with market participants who follow their every move). I hope it holds some appeal to both.

All authors are indebted. My indebtedness comes in different shapes and sizes. While preparing the earlier Marshall Lectures, I benefitted from the valued inputs of many members of the Fed's fine research staff. I hope I am not leaving anyone out when I mention Jon Faust, Richard Freeman, Dale Henderson, Karen Johnson, Ruth Judson, David Lindsey, Athanasios Orphanides, Vincent Reinhart, Peter Tinsley, and especially David Lebow, who was my special assistant at the Fed.

But, most of all, I gained enormously from a virtually continuous conversation with Janet Yellen while we both sat on the Federal Reserve Board. We served as sounding boards, confidants, and intellectual sparring partners for one another on an almost daily basis—so much so that, in many cases, I cannot remember whether a particular idea originated with me or with her.

I am also grateful for comments received at Cambridge University, at several other presentations of related materials, from Stanley Fischer, from Marvin Goodfriend, and from several anonymous reviewers of the manuscript.

But I would be remiss not to mention the substantial debt of gratitude I owe to my many friends and colleagues on the Federal Open Market Committee and at the central banks of other countries. Working with them was an education in the practical aspects of central banking which enriched my views on the issues in ways that are simply not attainable in a university setting.

Finally, my wife Madeline and I must acknowledge the marvelous hospitality of the staff of the LSE and of the Robbins family, which helped make my stay in London a pure joy—even though it rained!

Alan S. Blinder
Princeton, NJ
August 1997

Central Banking in
Theory and Practice

1

Targets, Instruments, and All That

1 Introduction

I realize that these are the Robbins lectures, not the Ricardo lectures. But please pardon a momentary digression on comparative advantage nonetheless, for I have long believed that one true test of whether a person is an economist is how devoutly he or she lives by the principle of comparative advantage. And I don't mean just *preaching* it, but actually *practicing* it. For example, I always harbor doubts about my economist friends who tell me that they mow their own lawns, rather than hiring a gardener, because they actually enjoy cutting grass. Such a claim is suspect on its face. But, more to the point, a true believer in comparative advantage should be constitutionally incapable of enjoying such activities; the David Ricardo inside him should make him feel too guilty.

As a devotee of comparative advantage, the topic of these lectures virtually chose itself. Our profession boasts greater economic theorists and more skilled econometricians than I. But there must be relatively few people on earth who have been as deeply immersed in monetary policy from both the academic and central banking sides as I have. Therein, I presume, lies my comparative advantage and the topic of these three lectures: the theory and practice of central banking.

To keep things manageable, I have pared the topic beyond what a literal reading of the title may suggest. First, central bankers, I can assure you, are busy with many matters that are related tangentially if at all to monetary policy—such as managing the payments system and supervising banks. But I will stick to monetary policy proper. Second, I will deal much more with the behavior of central banks than with the monetary transmission mechanism. In these lectures, short-term interest rates are more often left-hand than right-hand variables.

The various issues covered in these three lectures are parts of a mosaic that could be taken up in many different orders. But a lecturer must draw some boundary lines, artificial though they may be, in order to divide the subject matter into lecture-sized portions. This I have done in the following way. The first lecture deals mainly with a variety of complications that a practical central banker must confront in trying to implement the classical targets-instruments approach. This presentation begs two important questions that I will address in the second lecture: What policy instrument should the central bank use? And should it attempt discretionary policy at all, rather than just relying on a simple rule? Finally, the last lecture is devoted to various positive and, especially, normative aspects of central bank independence.

As these lectures progress, it will become apparent that central banking looks rather different in practice than it does in theory. Having seen it from both sides now, I deeply believe that both theory and practice could benefit from greater contact with and greater understanding of the other. Hence, I will periodically point out opportunities for cross-fertilization—places where central bankers have more to learn from academic research, and places where academic economists could profit from greater awareness of the practical world of central banking. Arbitrage should take care of the rest!

2 Targets and Instruments: The Rudiments

Monetary policymakers have certain objectives—such as low inflation, output stability, and perhaps external balance—and certain instruments to be deployed in meeting their responsibilities, such as bank reserves or short-term interest rates. Unless it has only a single goal,[1] the central bank is forced to strike a balance among competing objectives, that is, to face up to various *trade-offs*. Unless your education in economics is very thin (or very recent!), these two sentences immediately bring to mind Tinbergen (1952) and Theil (1961). So let us begin there, at the beginning.

In theory, it works like this. There is a known model of the macroeconomy, which I write in structural form as:

$$y = F(y,x,z) + e \tag{1}$$

and in reduced form as:

$$y = G(x,z) + e. \tag{2}$$

Here y is the vector of endogenous variables (a few of which are central bank objectives), x is the vector of policy instruments (which may be of size one), and z is the vector of nonpolicy exogenous variables. The vector e of stochastic disturbances will fade in importance once I assume, with Tinbergen and Theil, that $F(.)$ is linear and the policymaker's objective function,

$$W = W(y), \tag{3}$$

is quadratic. In principle, the policymaker maximizes the expected value of (3) subject to the constraint (2) to derive an optimal policy "rule":

$$x^* = H(z). \tag{4}$$

All very simple.

What's wrong with this simple framework? Both nothing and everything. Starting with "nothing," I do believe that—once you add a host of complications, several of which I will discuss in this lecture—this is the right way for a central banker to think about monetary policy. You have an economy. Except for the policy instruments you control, you must accept it as it is. You also have multiple objectives—your own, or those assigned to you by the legislature—and you must weigh them somehow, though perhaps not quadratically. To a significant extent, though usually quite informally and to my mind not quite sufficiently, central bankers do think about policy this way.

But, as is well known, there are many complications. Let me list just a few, some of which I will dwell on at length in the balance of this lecture and the next:

1. *Model uncertainty:* In practice, of course, we do not know the model but must estimate it econometrically. Since econo-

mists agree neither on the "right" model nor on the "right" econometric techniques, this is a nontrivial problem. It means, among other things, that policy multipliers—the derivatives of $G(.)$ with respect to x—are subject to considerable uncertainty.

2. *Lags:* Any reasonable macroeconometric model will have a complex lag structure that is ignored by (1). This is not much of a problem in principle because, as all graduate students learn, this complication can be accommodated formally simply by appending further equations for lagged variables (see Chow 1975). However, in practice it creates serious difficulties that bedevil policymakers.

3. *Need for forecasts:* Because of lags, execution of the Tinbergen–Theil framework requires forecasts of the future paths of the exogenous variables—in principle, the entire z vector, which may be quite long. Such forecasts are neither easy to generate nor particularly accurate.

4. *Choice of instrument:* The Tinbergen–Theil framework takes as given that some variables are endogenous and others are policy instruments. In most cases, however, the central bank has at least some latitude, and maybe quite a lot, in choosing its instrument(s). One way of thinking about this is that some of the xs and ys can trade places at the discretion of the central bank. For example, the short-term interest rate can be the policy instrument and bank reserves an endogenous variable; or the central bank can do things the other way around. Some economists take this idea a little too far and write models in which central bankers can control, say, nominal GDP, the inflation rate, or the

unemployment rate on a period-by-period basis. Believe me, they cannot. If they could, monetary policy would be a good deal simpler than it is.

5. *The objective function:* The next problem can be framed as a question: Who supplies the objective function? The answer, typically, is: no one. The political authorities, who after all should decide such things, rarely if ever give such explicit instructions to their central banks. So central bankers must—in a figurative, not literal, sense—create their own social welfare function based on their legal mandate, their own value judgments, and perhaps their readings of the political will. This last thought brings up the independence of the central bank—a subject I will take up in depth in the third lecture.

Adding it all up, a curmudgeon could summarize the problems with applying the Tinbergen–Theil program as follows: We do not know the model, and we do not know the objective function, so we cannot compute the optimal policy rule. To some critics of "impractical" or "theoretical" economics, including some central bankers, this criticism is a show-stopper. But, speaking now as a former central banker, I think such know-nothingism is not a very useful attitude. In fact, in my view, we must use the Tinbergen–Theil approach—with as many of the complications as we can handle—even if in a quite informal way. An analogy will explain why.

Consider your role as the owner of an automobile. You have various objectives toward which the use of your car contributes, such as getting to work, shopping, and going on pleasure trips. You do not literally "know" the utility function that weighs these objectives, but you presumably wish to maximize it nonetheless. The care and feeding of your car entails considerable expense, and you have great uncertainty about the "model" that maps inputs like gasoline, oil, and tires into outputs like safe, uneventful trips. Furthermore, there are substantial, stochastic lags between maintenance expenditures (e.g., frequent oil changes) and their payoff (e.g., greater engine longevity).

What do you do? One alternative is the "putting out fires" strategy: Do nothing for your car until it breaks down, then fix whatever is broken and continue driving until something else breaks down. I submit that few of us follow this strategy because we know it will produce poor results.[2] Instead, we all follow something that approximates—philosophically, if not mathematically—the Tinbergen–Theil framework. Central banks do, too. Or at least they should, for they will surely fail in their stabilization-policy mission if they simply "put out fires" as they observe them. Let me review briefly how the Tinbergen–Theil framework is used in practice.

To begin with, there must be a macro model. It need not be a system of several hundred stochastic difference equations, though that is not a bad place to start. In fact, no central bank that I know of, and certainly not the Federal Reserve, is wed to a single econometric model of its economy. Some banks have such models, and some do not. But, even if they do not, or do not use it, *some* kind of a model—however informal—is necessary to do policy, for otherwise how can you even begin to estimate the effects of changes in policy instruments?

Some central bankers scoff at large-scale macroeconometric models, as do some academic economists. And their reasons are not all that dissimilar. Many point, for example, to the likelihood of structural change in any economy over a period of several decades, which casts doubt on the stationarity assumptions that underlie standard econometric procedures and thus on the bedrock notion that the past is a guide to the future. Others express skepticism that something as complex as an entire economy can be captured in any set of equations. Still other critics emphasize a host of technical problems in time series econometrics that cast doubt on any set of estimated coefficients. Finally, some central bankers simply do not understand these ungainly creatures at all and doubt that they should be expected to.

Leaving aside the last, there is truth in each of these criticisms. Every model is an oversimplification. Economies do change over time. Econometric equations often fail subsample stability tests. Econometric problems like simultaneity, common trends, and omitted variables are ubiquitous in nonexperimental data. The Lucas critique warns us that some parameters may change when policy does.[3] Yet what are we to do about these problems? Be skeptical? Of course. Use several methods and models instead of just one? Certainly. But abandon all econometric modeling? I think not. The criticisms of macroeconometrics are not wrong, but their importance is often exaggerated and their implications misunderstood. These criticisms should be taken as warnings—as calls for caution, humility, and flexibility of mind—not as excuses to retreat into econometric nihilism. It is foolish to make the best the enemy of the moderately useful.

Indeed, I would go further. I don't see that central bankers even have the luxury of ignoring econometric estimates. Monetary policymaking requires more than just the qualitative information that theory provides—e.g., that if short-term interest rates rise, real GDP growth will subsequently fall. They must have quantitative information about magnitudes and lags, even if that information is imperfect.

I often put the choice this way: You can get your information about the economy from admittedly fallible statistical relationships, or you can ask your uncle. I, for one, have never hesitated over this choice. But I fear there may be altogether too much uncle-asking in government circles in general, and in central banking circles in particular. For example, a long line of politicians will assure you that a lower capital gains tax rate will spur investment. The only trouble is that no evidence supports this contention. Similarly, central bankers often take it as axiomatic that long-term interest rates are good forecasters of either (a) inflation or (b) future short-term interest rates. Unfortunately, the data refute both claims.

3 Uncertainties: Models and Forecasts

Let me now turn to the first of three important amendments to the Tinbergen–Theil framework, beginning with the obvious fact that no one knows the "true model." It would hardly have been news to Tinbergen and Theil that both models and forecasts of exogenous variables are subject to considerable uncertainties. And subsequent developments by economists have provided ways of handling or finessing these gaps in our knowledge.[4] Let us consider, very briefly, three types of uncertainty.

Uncertainty about forecasts: In the linear-quadratic case, uncertainty about the values of future exogenous variables is no problem *in principle;* you need only replace unknown future variables with their expected values (the "certainty equivalence" principle). But here is one case in which the gap between theory and practice is huge because the task of generating unbiased forecasts of dozens or even hundreds of exogenous variables is a titanic practical problem. It is, for example, a major reason why large-scale econometric models are not terribly useful as forecasting tools.[5]

Skeptics often object to certainty equivalence on the grounds that (a) the economy is nonlinear and (b) there is no particular reason to think that the objective function is quadratic. Both objections are undoubtedly true and, if taken literally, invalidate the certainty-equivalence principle. But I think the importance of this point is often exaggerated by those who would denigrate the usefulness—and thereby escape the discipline—of formal econometric models. Policymakers almost always will be contemplating changes in policy instruments that can be expected to lead to small changes in macroeconomic variables. For such changes, any model of an economy is approximately linear and any convex objective function is approximately quadratic.[6] So this problem of principle is, in my view, of great practical importance only on those rare occasions when large changes in policy are contemplated.

Uncertainty about parameters: Uncertainty about parameters, and hence about policy multipliers, is much more difficult to handle, even at the conceptual level. Certainty equivalence certainly does not apply. While there are some fairly sophisticated techniques for dealing with parameter uncertainty in optimal control models with learning, those methods have not attracted the attention of either macro-economists or policymakers. There is good reason for this inattention, I think: You don't conduct experiments on a real economy solely to sharpen your econometric estimates.

There is, however, one oft-forgotten principle that I suspect practical central bankers can—and in a rough way do—rely on. Many years ago, William Brainard (1967) demonstrated that, under certain conditions,[7] uncertainty about policy multipliers should make policymakers *conservative* in the following specific sense: They should compute the direction and magnitude of their optimal policy move in the way prescribed by Tinbergen–Theil and then do less.

Here is a trivial adaptation of Brainard's simple example. Simplify equation (2) to:

$$y = Gx + z + e, \tag{2'}$$

and suppose that G and z are independent random variables with means g and $\bar{z}$ respectively. The policymaker wishes to minimize $E(y - y^*)^2$. Interpret $z + e$ as the value of y in the absence of any further policy move ($x = 0$) and x as the contemplated change in policy.[8] If G is nonrandom, the optimal policy adjustment is certainty equivalence:

$$x = (y^* - \bar{z})/G,$$

that is, fully closing the expected gap between y^* and $\bar{z}$. But if G is random with mean g and standard deviation σ, the loss function is minimized by setting:

$$x = \frac{y^* - \overline{z}}{g + \dfrac{\sigma^2}{g}} \, ,$$

which means that policy aims to fill only part of the gap.

My intuition tells me that this finding is more general—or at least more wise—in the real world than the mathematics will support.[9] And I certainly hope it is, for I can tell you that it was never far from my mind when I occupied the Vice Chairman's office at the Federal Reserve. In my view as both a citizen and a policymaker, a little stodginess at the central bank is entirely appropriate.

Uncertainty over model selection: Parameter uncertainty, while difficult, is at least a relatively well defined problem. Selecting the right model from among a variety of non-nested alternatives is another matter entirely. While there is some formal literature on this problem,[10] I think it is safe to say that central bankers neither know nor care much about this literature. I leave it as an open question whether they are missing much.

My approach to this problem while on the Federal Reserve Board was relatively simple: Use a wide variety of models and don't ever trust any one of them too much. So, for example, when the Federal Reserve staff explored policy alternatives, I always insisted on seeing results from (a) our own quarterly econometric model, (b) several alternative econometric models, and (c) a variety of vector autoregressions (VARs) that I developed for this purpose. My usual procedure was to simulate a policy on as many of these models as possible, throw out the outlier(s), and average the rest to get a point estimate of a dynamic multiplier path.

This can be viewed as a rough—make that very rough—approximation to optimal information processing.[11] As they say: Good enough for government work!

4 Lags in Monetary Policy

It is a commonplace that monetary policy operates on the economy with "long and variable lags." As I noted previously, the formalism of the Tinbergen–Theil framework can readily accommodate distributed lags. The costs are two-fold. First, the dimensionality of the problem increases; but with modern computing power this is not much of a problem. Second, the optimization problem changes from one of calculus to one of dynamic programming.[12] This latter point is significant in practice and, I think, inadequately appreciated by practitioners.

A dynamic programming problem is typically "solved backward," that is, if T is the final period and x is the policy instrument, you first solve a one-period optimization problem for period T, thereby deriving $_tx_T$ conditional on a past history. (The postscript denotes calendar time and the prescript denotes the date at which the expectation is taken.) Then, given your solution for $_tx_T$, which most likely depends *inter alia* on $_tx_{T-1}$, you solve a two-period problem for $_tx_T$ and $_tx_{T-1}$ jointly. Proceeding similarly, by a process of backward induction you derive an entire *solution path*:

$$x_t,\ _tx_{t+1},\ _tx_{t+2},\ \ldots,\ _tx_T.$$

Don't get me wrong. I do not believe it is important for central bankers to acquire any deep understanding of Bellman's principle, still less of the computational techniques used to implement it. What really matters for sound decisionmaking is the way dynamic programming teaches us to think about intertemporal optimization problems—and the discipline it imposes. It is essential, in my view, for central bankers to realize that, in an dynamic economy with long lags in monetary policy, today's monetary policy decision must be thought of as the first step along a path. The reason is simple: Unless you have thought through your expected future actions, it is impossible to make today's decision rationally. For example, when a central bank begins a cycle of either tightening or easing, it should have some idea about where it is going before it takes the first step.

Of course, by the time period $t + 1$ rolls around, the policymaker will have new information and may wish to change his or her mind about the earlier tentative decision $_tx_{t+1}$. That is fine. In fact, given the information then available, the policymaker will want to plan an entirely new path:

$$x_{t+1}, {}_{t+1}x_{t+2}, {}_{t+1}x_{t+3}, \cdots, {}_{t+1}x_T$$

But that realization in no way obviates the need to think ahead in order to make today's decision—which is the important lesson of dynamic programming. It is an intensely practical lesson and, I believe, one that is inadequately understood.[13]

Too often decisions on monetary policy—and, indeed, on other policies—are taken "one step at a time" without any clear notion of what the next several steps are likely to be. In central banking circles, it is often claimed that such one-step-at-a-time decisionmaking is wise because it maintains "flexibility" and guards against getting "locked in" to decisions the central bank will later regret. I often heard sentiments like this expressed both at FOMC meetings and at international meetings of central bankers.

But this attitude reflects a fundamental misunderstanding of the way dynamic programming teaches us to think. It is absolutely correct that flexibility should be maintained and that locking yourself in should be avoided. But both of these notions are inherent in dynamic programming. If there are any surprises at all, the decisions that you actually carry out in the future will differ from the ones you originally planned. That's flexibility. Ignoring your own likely future actions is myopia.

These matters are really quite intuitive. Despite their lack of understanding of the fine points of the calculus of variations, ordinary rational people do not deem it wise to ignore the admittedly unknown future in order to "maintain flexibility." Think, for example, about students formulating educational and career plans. In choosing a major, and sometimes even in choosing a college, many undergraduates are looking ahead to their ultimate career objectives. They know their crystal ball is cloudy, and they realize that they may have many reasons to change their minds along the way. But they nonetheless find it rational to plan ahead when making the initial decision. And they are right.

Applying this abstract discussion to a concrete problem in monetary policy may help resolve a long-standing issue in central banking. Policymakers in the United States and elsewhere have often been accused of making a particular type of systematic error in the timing of policy changes. Specifically, it is alleged that they overstay their policy stance—whether it is tightening or loosening—thereby causing overshoots in both directions.[14] I believe this criticism may be correct, although I know of no systematic study that demonstrates it. I furthermore believe that the error, if it exists, may be due to following a strategy I call "looking out the window."

The error is well illustrated by what I call the parable of the thermostat. The following has probably happened to you; it has certainly happened to me. You arrive at night in an unfamiliar hotel and find the room temperature too cold. So you turn up the heat and take a shower. Emerging 10 minutes later, you still find the room too cold. So you turn the heat up another notch and go to sleep. At about 2 a.m. you wake up in a pool of sweat in a room that is oppressively hot.

By analogy, a central bank following the "looking out the window" strategy proceeds as follows. For concreteness, suppose it is in the process of tightening. At each decision-making juncture, the bank takes the economy's temperature and, if it is still too hot, tightens monetary conditions another notch. Given the long lags in monetary policy, you can easily see how such a strategy can keep the central bank tightening for too long.

Now compare "looking out the window" to proper dynamic optimization. Under dynamic programming, at each stage the bank would project an entire path of future monetary policy actions, with associated paths of key economic variables. It would, of course, act only on today's decision. Then, if things evolved as expected, it would keep following its projected path, which would be likely (given the lags in monetary policy) to tell it to stop tightening while the economy was still "hot." Of course, economies rarely evolve as expected. Surprises are the norm, not the exception, and they would induce the central bank to alter its expected path in obvious ways. If the economy steamed ahead faster than expected, the bank would tighten more. If the economy slowed down sooner than expected, the bank would tighten less or even reverse its stance.

Do central banks actually behave this way? Yes and no. Like a skilled billiards player who does not understand the laws of physics, a skilled practitioner of monetary policy may follow a dynamic-programming-type strategy intuitively and informally. In the last few years, for example, the notion that it is wise to pursue a strategy of "preemptive strikes" against inflation seems to have caught on among central bankers. The main impetus for this change in fashion was, I believe, the leadership and perceived success of the Federal Reserve in first tightening monetary policy "preemptively" in early 1994 and then achieving the fabled "soft landing." By now, a variety of other central banks are talking the same talk. But the very fact that this style of decision-making was perceived to be a great advance suggests that the dynamic programming way of thinking has not yet permeated central banking circles.

A preemptive strategy implies a certain amount of confidence in both your forecast and your model of how monetary policy affects the economy, both of which are hazardous. But preemption does not require too much confidence. Remember the flexibility principle of dynamic programming and the Brainard conservatism principle. Taken together, they lead to the following sort of strategy:[15]

Step 1. Estimate how much you need to tighten or loosen monetary policy to "get it right." Then do less.

Step 2. Watch developments.

Step 3a. If things work out about as expected, increase your tightening or loosening toward where you thought it should be in the first place.

Step 3b. If the economy seems to be evolving differently from what you expected, adjust policy accordingly.

Two final points about preemptive monetary policy are worth making. First, a successful stabilization policy based on preemptive strikes will appear to be misguided and may therefore leave the central bank open to severe criticism. The reason is simple. If the monetary authority tightens so early that inflation never rises, the preemptive strike is a resounding success, but critics of the central bank will wonder—out loud, no doubt—why the bank decided to tighten when the inflationary dragon was nowhere to be seen. Similarly, a successful preemptive strike against economic slack will prevent unemployment from rising and leave critics complaining that the authorities were hallucinating about rising unemployment. Precisely these criticisms of the Fed's tightening in 1994–1995 and subsequent easing in 1995–1996 were heard in the United States in recent years.

Second, the logic behind the preemptive strike strategy is symmetric. The same reasoning that tells a central bank to get a head start against inflation says it should also strike preemptively against rising unemployment. That is why Chairman Alan Greenspan told Congress in February 1995, just after the Fed had completed a year-long tightening cycle that raised short-term interest rates 300 basis points, that: "There may come a time when we hold our policy stance unchanged, or even ease, despite adverse price data, should we see signs that underlying forces are acting ultimately to reduce inflationary pressures."[16] In fact, the statement itself amounted to a monetary easing, since it fueled a bond-market rally well before the Fed started cutting interest rates (which did not occur until July 1995). Notably, both Greenspan's statement and the Fed's interest-rate cut in July 1995 came while the unemployment rate was below contemporary estimates of the natural rate.

Under what circumstances might the preemptive strike strategy apply more to fighting inflation than to fighting unemployment?

First, if the short-run Phillips curve is distinctly nonlinear in the way Phillips originally drew it, so that low unemployment raises inflation more than high unemployment lowers it. But, with due apologies to those notable curve-fitting exercises done at the London School of Economics in the 1950s, the U.S. evidence is decidedly against this hypothesis. A linear Phillips curve fits the data extremely well,[17] and tests for nonlinearity suggest, if anything, a concave (to the origin) Phillips curve rather than with a convex one.[18]

Second, the central bank's loss function could attach much more weight to inflation than to unemployment—as some observers of central banking have suggested, and as some central bank charters (but not the Fed's) mandate.

Third, lags in monetary policy could be longer for inflation fighting than for unemployment fighting, calling for earlier preemption in the former case. This last circumstance appears to obtain, and may be the main justification for acting more preemptively against inflation than against unemployment.

Note, however, that political considerations most likely point in the opposite direction. In most situations, the central bank will take far more political heat when it tightens pre-

emptively to avoid higher inflation than when it eases preemptively to avoid higher unemployment.

5 Central Banking by Committee

So far, I have offered one explanation for the alleged ten-
dency of central banks to overstay their stance—remaining
tight for too long, thereby causing recessions, and remaining
easy for too long, thereby allowing inflation to take root: a
failure to internalize the dynamic-programming way of
thinking. But a prominent institutional feature of some central banks (including the Federal Reserve) may also contribute to this problem. Specifically, in many countries monetary
policy is made not by a single individual but by a *committee.*

While serving on the FOMC, I was vividly reminded of a
few things all of us probably know about committees: that
they laboriously aggregate individual preferences; that they
need to be led; that they tend to adopt compromise positions
on difficult questions; and—perhaps because of all of the
above—that they tend to be inertial. Had Newton served on
more faculty committees at Cambridge, his first law of motion might have read: A decisionmaking body at rest or in
motion tends to stay at rest or in motion in the same direction unless acted upon by an outside force.

Inertial behavior has its virtues, as I will explain shortly.
But it also has some vices. In particular, decisionmaking by
committee may contribute to the systematic policy errors I
have mentioned already by inducing the central bank to
maintain its policy stance too long.

While the Federal Open Market Committee has not been
immune to this ailment over the years, there is at least one

tradition at the Federal Reserve that tends to minimize it: that of the powerful chairman. The law says that each of the 12 voting members of the FOMC has one vote. But no one has ever doubted that Alan Greenspan, or Paul Volcker, or Arthur Burns were "more equal" than the others. The Chairman of the Federal Reserve Board is virtually never on the losing side of a monetary policy vote. So, to a significant extent, FOMC decisions are *his* decisions, as tempered by the opinions of the other members. Nonetheless, a chairman who needs to build consensus may have to move more slowly than if he were acting alone.

Now for the positive side. America is the land of checks and balances. Our political traditions harbor great fear of unbridled, centralized power. It is an anti-government form of government—the little government that couldn't because it was too tied up in knots. Yet the Federal Open Market Committee has virtually total freedom to do as it pleases with monetary policy—without asking permission from any other branch of government and with little fear of being countermanded. So long as FOMC decisions are done by the book and remain within the Fed's legal authority, the committee is neither checked nor balanced—at least not externally.

But the group nature of FOMC decisions creates what amounts to an *internal* system of checks and balances. No chairman can deviate too far from the view that prevails in his committee. Decisionmaking by committee, especially when there is a strong tradition of consensus, makes it very difficult for idiosyncratic views to prevail.[19] So monetary policy decisions tend to regress toward the mean and to be inertial—and hence biased in just the same way that adaptive expectations are biased relative to rational expectations. But errors like that, while systematic, will generally be small and will tend to shrink over time. And, in return, the system builds in natural safeguards against truly horrendous mistakes.

I leave it to some clever theorist to prove that the FOMC is an example of optimal institutional design. My own hunch is that, on balance, the additional monetary policy inertia imparted by group decisionmaking provides a net benefit to society. It does, at least, provide something of a check against an overzealous Fed chairman. But my main point is simpler: My experience as a member of the FOMC left me with a strong feeling that the theoretical fiction that monetary policy is made by a single individual maximizing a well-defined preference function misses something important. In my view, monetary theorists should start paying some attention to the nature of decisionmaking by committee, which is rarely mentioned in the academic literature.[20]

6 Conclusion

Overall, however, the message of this lecture is rather cheerful. Working in their cloistered universities, Tinbergen, Theil, Brainard, and others taught valuable abstract lessons that turned out to be of direct practical use in central banking. So did other scholars who developed their ideas further, pointed out additional complexities, and brought more powerful technical tools to bear—such as macroeconometric models and dynamic programming. Their ideas do not provide pat answers for central bankers, and their techniques cannot be applied mechanically. The real world is much too complicated for that. So there must be both art and science in central banking. Nonetheless, the science is still useful; at least I found it so while on the Federal Reserve Board.

In fact, I think central bankers could learn a good deal more from the academics. For example, I emphasized that the dynamic programming way of thinking is not sufficiently ingrained into the habits of monetary policymakers, who too often just "look out the window" and base policy judgments on present circumstances. I believe this is a fundamental mistake and is one reason why central banks often overstay their policy stance.

There also seems to be much too much reliance on "uncle asking," relative to econometric evidence, among practical central bankers. Skepticism about econometric estimates is one thing, and is highly appropriate. But healthy skepticism should not be allowed to devolve into econometric nihilism, which is too often an excuse for wishful thinking and an escape from the discipline of the data.

But please don't think I believe that all wisdom resides in universities, from where it flows, somewhat impeded, to central banks. The next lecture should dispel that notion completely. After dealing briefly with one more issue where academic thinking was both correct and triumphant—the choice of monetary instrument—I will turn in detail to the rules versus discretion debate, where I will argue that much recent academic research has been barking up the wrong— or, rather, nonexistent—trees. On that issue, I believe, the academics must learn from the central bankers, and the sooner the better.

2   Choosing and Using a Monetary Policy Instrument

1 Introduction

In dealing with the pervasive uncertainties that surround monetary policy in the first lecture, I swept one very basic issue under the rug: What is the policy lever? What instrument does the central bank actually control?

The Tinbergen–Theil framework elides one of the most enduring controversies in monetary theory simply by labeling some variables as "targets" and others as "instruments," as if that were their birthright. Plainly, it is not. Central bankers all over the world must choose their policy instruments, so I begin this second lecture with a few thoughts on that choice. Although the ground is mostly well ploughed, I will introduce some new thoughts by proposing an answer to a question that has long bedeviled both practitioners and students of monetary policy: How do we define a "neutral" monetary policy?

The greater part of this lecture, however, will be devoted to an even more basic and contentious issue: whether it makes sense to attempt discretionary monetary policy at all, rather than rely on a simple mechanical rule—the age-old debate over rules versus discretion. Here, as I suggested at the end of the first lecture, I will be sharply critical of a large body of recent adacemic research which has, in my view, made insufficient contact with reality.

2 The Choice of Monetary Instrument

In simple models, beginning with Poole (1970), the choice of monetary instrument is often posed as a contest between the rate of interest, r, and the money supply, M. In one case, r is the instrument, and M is an endogenous variable. In the other case, the roles are reversed. This dichotomy, of course, is both too confining and too simple. In reality, there are many more choices—including various definitions of M, several possible choices for r, bank reserves, and the exchange rate. Furthermore, it is doubtful that any interesting definition of M or any interest rate beyond the overnight bank rate can be controlled tightly over very short periods of time like a day or a week. In the United States, the federal funds rate and bank reserves are probably the only viable options. But other variables like the Ms become candidates if the control period is longer—say, a quarter—and the control tolerances are wider.

The intellectual problem is straightforward in principle. For any choice of instrument, you can write down and solve an appropriately complex dynamic optimization problem, compute the minimized value of the loss function, and then select the *minimum minimorum* to determine the optimal policy instrument. In practice, this is a prodigious technical feat that is rarely carried out.[1] And I am pretty sure that no central bank has ever selected its instrument this way. But, then again, billiards players may practice physics only intuitively.

Returning to Poole's dichotomy, let me remind you of his basic conclusion: that large LM shocks militate in favor of targeting interest rates while large IS shocks militate in favor of targeting the money supply.[2] After Poole's seminal paper, monetary theorists devoted much attention to the question he posed and tackled it in a variety of ways. One such contribution by Sargent and Wallace (1975), in fact, turned out to be among the opening salvos in the rational expectations debate.

Much of the scholarly literature was worthwhile and intellectually fascinating. But in the end, real-world events, not theory, decided the issue. Ferocious instabilities in estimated LM curves in the United States, United Kingdom, and many other countries, beginning in the 1970s and continuing to the present day, led economists and policymakers alike to conclude that money-supply targeting is simply not a viable option. Some facts about the U.S. monetary aggregates illustrate just how strong this evidence is.

Surely the weakest version of monetarism must be the notion that money and nominal income are cointegrated, for with no such long-run relationship why would anyone care about the behavior of the Ms? Yet a series of cointegration tests for $M1$ and nominal GDP in the United States, using rolling samples of quarterly data beginning in 1948:1 and ending at various dates, fail to reject the hypothesis of no cointegration as soon as the endpoint of the sample extends into the late 1970s.[3] That is, the natural logs of $M1$ and nominal GDP are cointegrated only for sample periods like 1948–1975, not since then.

Apparent cointegration between either $M2$ or $M3$ on the one hand and nominal GDP on the other lasts longer. But it, too, disappears into a black hole in the 1990s. In fact, this statement is actually far too kind to $M2$ or $M3$ monetarism, since data limited to periods like 1948–1980 fail to indicate cointegration. A cointegrating vector appears only when the sample is extended well into the 1980s, but then it disappears again as data from the 1990s are appended. In a word, no sturdy long-run statistical relationship exists between nominal GDP and *any* of the Federal Reserve's three official definitions of M for *any* sample that includes the 1990s.

Because of stark facts like these, interest rate targeting won by default in the United States and elsewhere. As Gerry Bouey, a former governor of the Bank of Canada, put it, "We didn't abandon the monetary aggregates, they abandoned us." I often put the issue this way to economists with monetarist leanings (a vanishing breed, to be sure): If you want the Fed to target the growth rate of M, you must first answer two questions: which definition of M, and how fast should it grow? In recent years, these questions have proven to be show-stoppers—for no one has coherent answers.

The death of monetarism does not make it impossible to pursue a monetary policy based on rules. But it does mean that the rule cannot be a money-growth rule. I will return to the broader rules-versus-discretion debate shortly.

Was the theoretical literature on the choice of monetary instrument therefore useless to practitioners? Absolutely not. In fact, it is hard to think of an aspect of monetary policy in which theory and practice have interacted more fruitfully. Poole's conclusion in theory was that instability in the LM curve should push central banks toward targeting short-term interest rates. In practice, LM curves became extremely unstable and one central bank after another abandoned any attempt to target monetary aggregates.

In the case of the Federal Reserve, the brief and tumultuous experiment with monetarism between 1979 and 1982 was probably more a marriage of convenience than infatuation. Monetarist rhetoric provided the Fed with a political heat shield as it raised interest rates to excruciating heights. In any case, the Fed began the gradual process of backing away from M targets in 1982. The target growth range for $M1$ was formally dropped in 1987, but growth targets for $M3$ and, especially, $M2$ retained some subsidiary role in monetary policy formulation into 1992—at least putatively. Finally, in February 1993, Fed Chairman Alan Greenspan announced with magnificent understatement that the Fed was giving "less weight to monetary aggregates as guides to policy."[4] Less? How about zero? Greenspan's proclamation was greeted with yawns in both academia and the financial markets because it was considered old news.

As usual, however, laws lag far behind both academic knowledge and central bank practice. The Humphrey–Hawkins Act, a 1978 law which is still on the books, requires the Federal Reserve to report its target ranges for money growth to Congress twice a year. This the Fed dutifully does. But it is an empty ritual. The relevance to policy eludes all concerned.

3 Real Interest Rates and "Neutral" Monetary Policy

So interest rates won by default. But what interest rate should the monetary authority try to control? And can it succeed?

Most empirically-oriented economists would agree with the following proposition, which seems to pose a major dilemma for monetary policy: The interest-sensitive components of aggregate demand react mainly to the real long rate while the central bank controls only the nominal short rate. In other words, the interest rate that the central bank can control doesn't matter (much), and the rates that really matter cannot be controlled. On the surface, this seems a devastating conundrum. But things are not quite as bad as they appear.

Note that two separate distinctions are being made here: nominal interest rates are not real rates, and short rates are not long rates. In this lecture, I would like to focus on the real-nominal distinction. So I hope you will grant me the liberty to proceed under the assumption that the expectations theory of the term structure appropriately links long rates to short rates—a convenient fiction that I will debunk in the following lecture.

In the contemporary United States, virtually all academic and market observers agree that the Federal funds rate—the overnight rate in the interbank market for reserves—is the Federal Reserve's central policy instrument.[5] And so does the Fed. But the Federal funds rate is, of course, a nominal rate, which means that the FOMC must act nominal while thinking real. Fortunately, this bit of mental gymnastics is not too hard to perform in the short run because inflationary expectations are, under normal circumstances, quite sluggish. So the Fed can be reasonably confident that short-run changes in the nominal Fed funds rate signify changes in the real Fed funds rate.

In the long run, however, telling the two apart is not so simple; and mistakes, if uncorrected, can be terribly damaging. The reason has been well known for years. Suppose that, in choosing a nominal interest rate, the central bank mistakenly sets the real interest rate too high. Such an error will restrict aggregate demand, eventually open up a GDP gap, and, with a lag, start to bring inflation down. If the central bank fails to adjust its nominal interest rate downward as inflation falls, the real rate will grow even larger. This spells trouble. The GDP gap expands, inflation falls faster, and real rates rise even more. The economy is put into a disinflationary tailspin.

The opposite happens if the nominal interest rate is accidentally pegged at a level that makes the real interest rate too low. In that case, loose monetary policy eventually leads to an overshoot of potential GDP and, thereby, to higher inflation. If the central bank holds the nominal interest rate fixed as inflation rises, the real rate falls even lower, aggregate demand gets stimulated even more, and the economy is off to the inflationary races.

The moral of the story is simple: Stubbornly pegging the nominal interest rate while inflation is changing (in either direction) is likely to be hazardous to your economy's health. Before too long, the central bank must adjust its nominal rate so as to guide the real rate back toward its *neutral* setting.

What was that word again? Neutral? I must pause a moment to examine a concept that is prominent in the financial press these days, even though it has no agreed-upon definition: the *neutral real interest rate*. Let me first propose a definition, and then defend it.[6]

At any point in time, given all the standard determinants of aggregate demand—including fiscal policy, the exchange rate, and the spending propensities of consumers and investors—the economy has some *steady-state IS curve*. By this I mean the IS curve that will prevail once all the lags have worked themselves out, and provided all random shocks are set to zero. Specifically, if the normal IS curve is written:

$$y = f(y_{-1}, r, x, G, \dots) + e,$$

the steady-state IS curve is:

$$y = f(y, r, x, G, \dots).$$

It is labelled "IS" in figure 2.1.

I propose to define the neutral real interest rate, r^*, as the interest rate that equates GDP along this steady-state IS curve to potential GDP, y^*; implicitly:

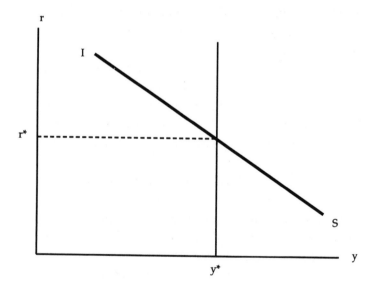

Figure 2.1
The neutral real interest rate

$$y^* = f(y^*, r^*, x, G, \dots).$$

Graphically, it is defined by the point in the graph at which the steady-state IS curve intersects the vertical line at potential GDP. Notice several critical features of this definition.

First, if the real interest rate is below the neutral rate, aggregate demand will eventually exceed potential GDP, leading to higher inflation. Conversely, a real interest rate above neutral will ultimately be disinflationary. Thus the proposed definition of neutrality is oriented entirely toward the control of inflation, as seems appropriate given that price stability is the primary long-run responsibility of any central bank. According to my proposed definition, "neutral" monetary policy is consistent with constant inflation in the medium run. Any higher real interest rate constitutes "tight money" and will eventually imply falling inflation; and any lower real rate is "easy money" and signals eventually rising inflation.

Second, the neutral real interest rate is not a fixed number. It depends, among other things, on fiscal policy and the exchange rate; and it is sensitive to other permanent (though not temporary) IS shocks. I use the steady-state IS curve to define the neutral real interest rate precisely to filter out transitory fluctuations in demand and focus on longer-run factors. But durable IS shocks do change the neutral rate.

Third, and implicit in what I just said, the neutral real rate of interest is difficult to estimate and impossible to know with precision. It is therefore most usefully thought of as a concept rather than as a number, as a way of thinking about monetary policy rather than as the basis for a mechanical rule.

But it is an operational concept. There are two main ways to get an estimate. One is to solve a complete macroeconometric explicitly for its neutral rate. Different econometric models will, of course, produce different numerical estimates; so alternative models should be examined. Bomfim (1997) has used the MPS model, the model formerly used at the Federal Reserve Board, to compute a quarterly time series on the neutral real federal funds rate based on a definition similar to mine. The key difference is that Bomfim uses the equation residuals to estimate the random shocks buffeting the economy and allows them to move the neutral rate up or down, whereas my definition sets the shocks to zero. The result is a time series that is quite volatile from quarter to quarter. According to his estimates, the neutral real funds rate has averaged about 2.8% during the 1990s.[7] It was typically much higher during the 1980s.

The other method is to compute the average *ex post* real rate over a long historical period—the idea being that lags work themselves out, transitory phenomena fade, and random shocks average to zero over long periods of time. Care must be taken, however, to avoid short periods that might be unrepresentative—as during the 1970s, when real interest rates were often negative, or the 1980s, when they were extraordinarily high. I prefer to use 30–50 years in computing such historical averages. This method tends to produce estimates of the neutral real federal funds rate in the 1.75–2.25% range, depending on the precise period chosen and the measure of inflation used to convert the nominal rate into a real rate.

My suggestion, then, is that central banks estimate the neutral real interest rate on a regular basis (a range may make more sense than a point estimate), and use that estimate as the "zero point" on their monetary policy scales. Any higher interest rate constitutes "tight money"; any lower rate constitutes "easy money." Neutrality is the only viable policy setting for the long run.

To tie these ideas to real events, consider Federal Reserve policy since the 1990–1991 recession. Gradually and, some might say, grudgingly, the Fed lowered the federal funds rate to 3%—which was about zero in real terms—in a lengthy series of steps culminating in the fall of 1992. As zero is well below the neutral rate by anyone's reckoning, monetary policy was clearly very stimulative. With a lag, the U.S. economy responded. Then, in February 1994, the Fed started moving the funds rate back toward neutral— explicitly calling attention to that concept as part of its justification. The nominal funds rate eventually peaked at 6%—which translated into a real rate slightly above 3%—in February 1995. That would be on the "tight" side of neutral by most—though not necessarily all—estimates. And the Fed held that rate until July 1995, when it began a three-step easing that brought Federal funds down to 5.25% on the last day of January 1996. With inflation running in the 2.5%–3% range, that meant a real rate between 2.25% and 2.75%— which was probably either neutral or just slightly on the tight side. Chairman Alan Greenspan explicitly acknowledged this in Congressional testimony in February 1997, when he said: "The real funds rate might be at a level that will promote continued non-inflationary growth."[8] But a month later he hedged his bet by nudging the Federal funds rate up another 25 basis points, where it remained as this book went to press.

4 The Rules versus Discretion Debate: Then and Now

Now that we have settled on a monetary policy instrument—the estimated real short-term rate of interest, it is time to face up to the really big question: Should the central bank use that instrument actively to try to stabilize the macroeconomy? Or should it rely passively on a rule?

Academic economists have long argued about whether central bankers practicing discretionary monetary policy should be replaced by a computer programmed to follow a mechanical rule. To my knowledge, practical central bankers have not joined this debate—presumably because they think they know the answer. As a former central banker, I naturally take the side of the establishment. But it is documented that I held this view even before I was admitted to the temple and learned the secret handshake.[9]

Before proceeding further, I must clarify what I mean by a *monetary policy rule,* to at least make clear what we are arguing about.

What Is a Rule?

The Tinbergen–Theil program that was discussed in the previous lecture will, if carried out, lead to a policy *reaction function* relating the central bank's instrument to a variety of independent variables—most prominently, the deviations of target variables from their desired levels. For example, the equation might have the overnight bank rate on the left and such items as inflation, unemployment, and the exchange rate or current account deficit on the right.

That is *not* what I mean by a rule. Rather, such an equation is, to me, a mathematical—and somewhat allegorical—representation of discretionary policy. It is the way an economist theorizing in the Tinbergen–Theil tradition imagines monetary policy to be made. To qualify as a rule, in my parlance, the "equation" for monetary policy must be simple and non-reactive, or nearly so. Friedman's famous k-percent rule is the best-known example, although holding money growth to a constant rate is no mean trick in the short run. Pegging the exchange rate is another realistic example. Holding the real short-term interest rate at its neutral level, no matter what, would be a third.

There is, however, another case that has gained prominence in the theoretical literature: assigning the central bank a rule based on *outcomes*, rather than one (like Friedman's) based on *instruments*. The two most obvious such rules are targeting inflation and targeting nominal GDP growth.

There is indeed an intellectual case for a rule of this sort. In fact, such rules come fairly close to—and in some cases duplicate—the legal mandates of central banks. The problem is that they are not really rules at all, but rather, objectives that may require a great deal of discretion to achieve. A government that wants to, say, stabilize the inflation rate at 2% cannot replace its central bank by a computer and throw away the key. Reaching that target and staying there is sure to require human judgment and adaptation to changing circumstances—to wit, discretion. The harsh but simple fact is that no central bank directly controls inflation, unemployment, or nominal GDP—much as economic theorists would like to pretend otherwise.

So, to me, the operational question is: Would it be better to replace central bank discretion with a simple rule based on instruments the bank can actually control, not on outcomes that it cannot control? Two very different lines of reasoning have been used to answer this question in the affirmative.

The Old Debate and the New Debate

The old-fashioned approach is intimately linked to the name Milton Friedman. Friedman and others argued that the automatic servo-mechanism of an unregulated economy would produce tolerably good, though certainly not perfect, results. While activist stabilization policy might be able to improve upon these results in principle, they doubt it will prove efficacious in practice because policymakers lack the knowledge, competence, and perhaps even the fortitude necessary to carry out the task. Faced with a choice between an imperfect economy and an imperfect government, Friedman and his followers opt without hesitation for the former. They share Lord Acton's concerns about power more than Lord Keynes's concerns about unemployment.

The arguments on each side of this old debate have been hashed over numerous times, so I will not repeat them here. Suffice it to say that, while I find the Friedmanite arguments for rules less than persuasive, they cannot be summarily dismissed. Our knowledge is indeed not quite up to snuff, and many monetary authorities have failed to acquit themselves with distinction. In all honesty, we must admit that there is at least an outside chance that Friedman could be right. However, I mention this older debate not to take sides but rather to contrast it with the newer version of the rules-versus-discretion debate.

The new arguments for rules take an entirely different tack. They are based neither on the ignorance nor the knavery of public officials and, in fact, assume that everyone knows how the economy operates—even the government! Moreover, the government's objectives are assumed to coincide with the people's objectives, and everyone has rational expectations. Despite these seemingly ideal circumstances, modern critics argue that a central bank left with discretion will err systematically in the direction of excessive inflation. To remedy this distortion, they advocate a fixed rule.

Kydland and Prescott (1977) initiated this new round of discourse by observing that the expectational Phillips curve poses a temptation to the monetary authorities. Specifically, by stimulating aggregate demand and surprising the private sector with unanticipated inflation, the central bank can reduce unemployment temporarily. Lower unemployment is prized by both the public and the central bank. The problem is that you can go to this well only so often and, under rational expectations, not very often at all.

If expectations are rational, people understand the central bank's behavior pattern, and monetary policy cannot produce systematic gaps between actual and expected inflation. So a central bank that regularly reaches for short-term gains will, on average, produce more inflation but no more employment than a central bank that is more resolute. But any central bank that makes monetary policy on a period-by-period discretionary basis will constantly face, and presumably succumb to, the temptation to reach for short-term gains. Kydland and Prescott dubbed this (an example of) the problem of *time inconsistency* and suggested that the way to solve it is to tie the central bankers' hands with a rule.

Barro and Gordon (1983a, 1983b) and Barro (1986) clarified this message and extended it in a variety of ways, noting among other things that the rule could be reactive and exploring the role of reputation as a way to produce less inflationary policies in repeated games. Their analyses spawned a small growth industry that spins theories of central bank behavior and offers remedies for the alleged inflationary bias of discretionary monetary policy. As an academic, I found this analysis unpersuasive. And what I learned as a central banker strongly reinforced this view. Let me explain why.

Three Major Objections

First, a historic point is worth making. With some variations in timing, the period from the mid-1960s until about 1980 was one of accelerating inflation in the industrial countries. Barro and Gordon ignored the obvious *practical* explanations for the observed upsurge in inflation—the Vietnam War, the end of the Bretton–Woods system, two OPEC shocks, and so on—and sought instead a *theoretical* explanation for what they believed to be a systematic inflationary bias in the behavior of central banks.[10] They found it in Kydland and Prescott's analysis.

But that was then and this is now. Recent history has not been kind to the view that central banks have an inflationary bias. In fact, the history of much of the industrial world since roughly 1980 has been one of disinflation—sometimes sharp disinflation, and sometimes at high social cost. Furthermore, the monetary authorities of many countries, especially in Europe, have displayed a willingness to maintain their tough anti-inflation stances to this very day, despite low inflation and persistently high unemployment. Whether or not you applaud these policies, they hardly look like grabbing for short-term employment gains at the expense of inflation.

How are we to reconcile the disinflation history of 1980–1997 with a theory that says that central banks systematically produce too much inflation? My answer is simple: We cannot. Nor can we dismiss the 1980–1997 period as a brief interlude of history, insufficiently long to belie the Barro–Gordon analysis, for the 1965–1980 period they used as "evidence" of inflationary bias was even shorter. Furthermore, few theorists seem to have noticed the following embarrassing fact: If the key parameters of the model are constant, the theory predicts stable inflation that is too high, not accelerating inflation. So it doesn't even explain the history of 1965–1980. The real question about that period is why inflation rose in so many countries. What changed?

I am tempted to conclude that Barro and Gordon and their followers were theorizing—and incorrectly at that—about the last war just as real-world central bankers were fighting the next one. In addition, it is worth noting that the real-world cure to the alleged "inflation bias" problem did not come from adopting rigid precommitment ("rules") or other institutional changes,[11] as Kydland–Prescott and Barro–Gordon suggested. It came from determined but discretionary application of tight money. Rather than seeking short-term gains, central banks paid the price to disinflate. As in the Nike commercial, they just did it.

My second objection is simple and practical: Most of the literature presumes that the central bank controls either the inflation rate or the unemployment rate perfectly on a period-by-period basis. Obviously, this is not so in reality. Now, a theorist may argue that this is an inessential point; after all, no theory is meant to be literally true. But I think that retort dismisses the objection too cavalierly. When the literature comes to discussing solutions to the inflationary-bias problem, as I will shortly, the arguments for simple rules based on outcomes (like "keep inflation at zero") or for certain incentive-based contracts seem to hinge sensitively on the notion that either the central bank controls inflation perfectly or that shocks are perfectly verifiable *ex post*. Trust me; the real world is not that simple. When the inflation rate changes, the public cannot be sure that the central bank did it. Come to think of it, neither can the bank!

My third objection appears to be a narrow technical detail, but it is not. The literature derived from Barro and Gordon (1983a) posits a loss function in inflation and unemployment that looks something like the following:

$$L = (u_t - ku^*)^2 + \alpha\pi^2_t,$$

where π_t is the inflation rate, u is the unemployment rate, u^* is the natural rate, α is a "taste" (or inflation-aversion) parameter, and k is a constant less than one indicating that the optimal unemployment rate is below the natural rate.[12] This last parameter turns out to be essential to the argument for inflationary bias. In fact, the inflationary bias of discretionary policy disappears in most models if $k = 1$.

I can assure you that it would not surprise my central banker friends to learn that economic theories that model them as seeking to drive unemployment below the natural rate imply that their policies are too inflationary. They would no doubt reply, "Of course that would be inflationary. That's why we don't do it." That reply points to a disarmingly simple solution to the Kydland–Prescott problem: *Direct* the central bank to aim for u^* rather than ku^*. That is exactly what I felt duty-bound to do while I was Vice Chairman of the Fed. And my attitude was hardly unique on the FOMC, where members were always concerned about the potential inflationary consequences of pushing unemployment below the natural rate.

Three Proposed Solutions

Let me now examine three proposed "solutions" to the inflationary-bias problem found in the theoretical literature. My purpose in each case is to compare theory to reality.

1. Reputation: The first solution hinges on notions of reputation—a concept, that is near and dear to the hearts of real central bankers. Here theorists have been barking up the right tree. Nonetheless, theoretical models of reputation have some peculiar features.

Consider, for example, Barro's (1986) model, in which the central banker is either a "tough guy," who will always opt for low inflation, or a "wet," who is willing to deviate in order to boost employment. The public does not know which kind of central banker it has, and is therefore forced into statistical inference. If the central bank keeps inflation low, its reputation—technically, the subjective probability that it is tough—will rise. This part rings true. For example, the Federal Reserve probably had relatively little anti-inflation credibility in the late 1970s but has quite a lot now. In Europe, I believe the monetary authorities of both the United Kingdom and France have built up substantial anti-inflation capital during the 1990s.

But in the model, as soon as the bank allows high inflation, even once, the public concludes—with certainty—that it is a hopeless "wet." This is the feature of the model that strikes me as eccentric, if not downright silly. In reality, there are many types of central banker, not just two, and random shocks cloud the mapping from outcomes back to types. For these and other reasons, reputation is not like pregnancy: You *can* have either a little or a lot. For example, the Bundesbank's entire reputation as an enemy of inflation did not collapse when German inflation rose from about zero in 1986 to about 4% in 1992. Nor should it have.

In central banking circles, it is viewed as obvious that the accumulation and destruction of reputational capital more closely resembles adaptive than rational expectations—it lags behind reality. Here, I think, the central bankers are closer to the truth than the economic theorists.

2. Principal-agent contracts: A second proposed cure for the alleged inflationary bias of monetary policy that has attracted the recent attention of theorists is drawing up a contract between the central bank as agent and the political authorities (which I shall parochially call "Congress") as principal. The genesis of the idea is simple. The Kydland–Prescott analysis suggests that the incentives of decision-makers are distorted toward excessive inflation. Say the word "distortion" and economists reflexively think of taxes and subsidies. So Walsh (1995) and Persson and Tabellini (1993) have proposed making the central banker's salary decline in proportion to inflation.[13] They show that this particular incentive scheme induces the central banker to behave optimally in the context of a model like that of Barro and Gordon (1983a).

What's wrong with this idea? Well, to start with, a small decrease in salary is probably not much of a motivator for central bankers who are already voluntarily giving up a large portion of their potential earnings to do public service. Let me put it bluntly and personally. When I was at the Fed, I had (more or less) a Walsh-type contract: Since my nominal salary was fixed by Congress and extremely unlikely to be raised, I suffered a 1% real wage loss for each point of U.S. inflation. But that meagre $1231 never once entered my thinking about monetary policy. It was dwarfed by my other financial losses. And I was just a fugitive from academia! Imagine the financial losses of a banker or successful business person.

Second, we must face up to the embarrassing fact that virtually no central bank explicitly ties its salaries to economic performance—not even New Zealand, where there really is a formal contract between the governor of the Reserve Bank and the minister of finance. The governor may be dismissed (and thus suffer a huge pay increase!) if inflation comes in too high. But he does not have his salary docked.

Third, and finally, there is a severe problem with the party on the other side of the contract.[14] In practice, "the public" cannot serve as the principal in the contemplated contract, so Congress must play this role as surrogate. But Congress is really an *agent*, not a principal. And members of Congress—who must stand for reelection—face even stronger incentives to reach for short-term gains than do central bankers. So why would Congress propose a contract with the central bank that would eliminate the inflationary bias? And, more important, why would it want to enforce such a contract if the central bank deviated and thereby caused a little boom?

Critics of government everywhere complain that elected officials focus myopically on the next election rather than on the best long-run interests of the nation. Indeed, that is probably the principal rationale for making the central bank independent from politics, as I will note in the next lecture. The vision of highly disciplined and farsighted politicians curing the wayward ways of profligate and myopic central bankers seems a strange role reversal. In the real world, it is independent central bankers who prevent politicians from succumbing to the Kydland–Prescott temptation.

3. *Conservative central bankers:* This brings me to the third proposed theoretical solution to the conundrum posed by Barro and Gordon—the one with the most practical appeal. Rogoff (1985) cleverly suggested that, if there is an inflationary bias in monetary policy, the cure may lie in the appointment of more "conservative" central bankers. Now that really does have the ring of truth! Indeed, in the real world the noun "central banker" practically cries out for the adjective "conservative."

To Rogoff, conservatism has a very specific meaning. In the Barro–Gordon model, the taste parameter α, which indicates the relative disutilities of inflation and unemployment, is presumed to be common to the central bank and the public. Rogoff suggested that politicians should deliberately select central bankers who are *more inflation averse* than society as a whole. That way, one bias (the unrepresentative preferences of the central bank) can cancel out the other (dynamic inconsistency).

Rogoff's model is a splendid illustration of the humorous definition of an economist as someone who sees that something works in practice and asks whether it can also work in theory. Is there any doubt that central banks in general and successful inflation-fighting central banks in particular have been dominated by quite conservative people? Rogoff's model argues that this common practice is wise. He may be right. Nonetheless, a few points about his proposed solution are worth making.

First, the enhanced vigilance against inflation produced by conservative central bankers comes at a cost: Real output and employment are more variable than in the dynamically inconsistent solution. That is fine because it presumably moves society closer to the optimum. My point is just that the gains on the inflation front come at some cost. Appointing conservatives to the central bank board does not buy society a free lunch.[15]

Second, you can have too much of a good thing. In Rogoff's model—and, I believe, in reality—it is possible to appoint a central banker who is too conservative, that is, whose value of the parameter α is so high that he or she does not deliver the combination of inflation and output variability that society really wants. Specifically, such a central bank will fight inflation too vigorously and be insufficiently mindful of the short-run employment costs. This too rings true, though I will refrain from naming names. It suggests that there is an optimal type of person best suited to a central bank board.

Third, Lohmann (1992) suggested an interesting amendment to the Rogoff approach which improves upon the solution—but one which must be handled with care. There may be times when it is optimal for the government to overrule the decision of the conservative central banker—for example, following a large supply shock. Lohmann suggests that such actions should be allowed, but only if the government pays a cost. In reality, the cost might be, e.g., the political heat the minister of finance would take if he or she overruled an important decision of the central bank governor. For example, the governor might resign in a huff.

Lohmann's idea is correct in both economic theory and political theory. In a democracy there should, after all, be some checks on the behavior of an over-zealous central bank. But its practical application is tricky, to say the least. No central bank can claim to be independent if its monetary policy decisions are routinely reversed. This remedy must be reserved for truly extraordinary circumstances. So any real-world government that adopts the Lohmann amendment must ensure that politicians overrule the central bank very rarely—for example, by making central bankers removable only for gross negligence. In the United States, Federal Reserve governors are removable by the president only for cause, and an act of Congress can overrule a Federal Reserve decision. But these are grave steps that have never been taken. In practice, Fed decisions are final.

The Bottom Line?

So where does this extended discussion of rules versus discretion leave us in the real, as opposed to the theoretical, world?

While Kydland and Prescott's insight points to a genuine difficulty for monetary policy, and some of the subsequent literature has been enlightening, there is less there than meets the eye. If there is strong agreement on both the positive aspects of a time-inconsistency problem (e.g., the Phillips curve) and its normative aspects (e.g., the social welfare function), as Barro and Gordon assume for the inflation problem, societies should have little difficulty in "solving" it, albeit imperfectly. For example, I just suggested one simple solution: *directing* the central bank to behave as if it prefers u^* rather than ku^*.

In fact, nations and households seem to find simple, practical ways to cope with a wide variety of potential dynamic inconsistencies—ways that bear little resemblance to the solutions suggested by theorists. Some common examples are dealing with flood plains, avoiding capital levies, punishing your children when they misbehave, and giving final examinations in courses. In each case, governments, parents, or teachers cope with a potential time-inconsistency problem, by creating—and then usually following—norms of behavior, by building reputations, and by remembering that there are many tomorrows. Rarely does society solve a time-inconsistency problem by rigid precommitment or by creating incentive-compatible compensation schemes for decisionmakers. Enlightened discretion is the rule.

Similarly, the revealed preferences of many democratic societies are to deal with the problem of dynamic inconsistency in monetary policy by legislating a long-term goal for the central bank (e.g., price stability), giving discretion to nonpolitical central bankers who have long time horizons and an aversion to inflation, and then hoping for the best. This is not obviously a bad solution.

5 Conclusion

The overall subject of these lectures is the interaction between academic theories of monetary policy and actual central bank practice. This lecture deals with three issues with very different resolutions.

In the case of choosing between interest rates and monetary aggregates as the policy instrument, the symbiosis was extremely strong. Academic research, beginning with Poole (1970), offered up sound and usable advice; and practical central bankers took it, to the benefit of all. Life imitated art.

In the case of the modern incarnation of the rules versus discretion debate, based on time inconsistency, I have argued that things are starkly different. In my view, the academic literature has focused on either the wrong problem or a nonproblem and has proposed a variety of solutions (excluding Rogoff's conservative central bankers) that make little sense in the real world. Unsurprisingly, they have had little influence on central banking practice. Here art would be well advised to imitate life a bit more.

The third issue—the choice of the zero point to define "neutral" monetary policy—is still unresolved. I have suggested using an estimated *neutral* real rate of interest, defined as the real short rate that is consistent with constant inflation, as the dividing line between "tight" and "loose" monetary policy. Neither the scholarly nor the practical jury has yet had enough time to consider and rule on this proposal. But I believe in market tests and am willing to wait for the verdict.

3   Central Bank Independence

1 Introduction

The first two lectures deal mainly with what might be called the *staples* of the theory of monetary policy as taught in universities—classic issues such as lags and uncertainties, the choice of monetary instrument, rules versus discretion, and so on. In concluding this series, I want to focus on central banking proper—viewing the central bank as an economic and, to some extent, a political institution. The issues for this final lecture involve economic considerations, to be sure. But they also have philosophical, organizational, and practical aspects that arise less frequently in economic discourse. I begin with the idea of central bank independence.

2 Central Bank Independence: Definition and Rationale

Everything, it seems, runs in fads. Lately, it appears, the trend has been toward greater central bank independence. But the term itself is somewhat vague and has occasionally been misused. So it may be useful to start with a definition.

To me, central bank independence means two things: first, that the central bank has freedom to decide how to pursue its goals and, second, that its decisions are very hard for any other branch of government to reverse. A few words on each are in order.

When I say that an independent central bank has considerable latitude to decide how to pursue its goals, that does not mean that the bank can select the goals by itself. On the contrary, in a democracy it seems entirely appropriate for the political authorities to set the goals and then instruct the central bank to pursue them. If it is to be independent, the bank must have a great deal of discretion over how to use its instruments to pursue its legislated objectives. But it need not have the authority to set the goals itself and, indeed, I would argue that giving the bank such authority would be an inappropriately broad grant of power. The elected representatives of the people should make such decisions. The central bank should then serve the public will. In the terminology suggested by Fischer (1994), the bank should have *instrument* independence but not *goal* independence.

So, for example, the Bundesbank is directed by law to "safeguard the currency," and the Federal Reserve is instructed to pursue both "maximum employment" and "stable prices."[1] In each case, the goals of monetary policy are set forth in legislation but are sufficiently imprecise that they require considerable interpretation by the central bank. Taking the Federal Reserve as an example, the so-called dual mandate requires the Fed to give tacit or explicit content to the vague phrases "maximum employment" and "stable prices" and then to decide how to deal with the short-run trade-off between the two. This interpretative role enhances the Fed's *de facto* power, which is considerable. But it is quite possible to have a highly independent central bank with more precisely defined goals; the numerical inflation target of the Reserve Bank of New Zealand is a case in point.

The second—and critical—hallmark of independence is near irreversibility. In the American system of government, for example, neither the President nor the Supreme Court can countermand the decisions of the Federal Open Market Committee (FOMC). Congress can, but only by passing a law that the President signs (or by overriding his veto). This makes FOMC decisions, for all practical purposes, immune from reversal. Without this immunity, the Fed would not really be independent, for its decisions would hold only so long as they did not displease someone more powerful.

Having defined independence, let me now pose a naive but crucial question: *Why should the central bank be independent?* The essence of my answer is disarmingly simple. Monetary policy, by its very nature, requires a long time horizon. One reason is that the effects of monetary policy on output and inflation come with long lags, so decision-makers do not see the results of their actions for quite some time. But the other, and far more important, reason is that disinflation has the characteristic cost-benefit profile of an investment activity: It costs something up front and pays back only gradually over time.

But politicians in democratic—and even undemocratic—countries are not known for either patience or long time horizons. Neither is the mass media nor the public. And none of these constituencies have much understanding of the long lags in monetary policy. So, if politicians made monetary policy on a day-to-day basis, the temptation to reach for short-term gains at the expense of the future (that is, to inflate too much) would be hard to resist. Knowing this, many governments wisely try to depoliticize monetary policy by, e.g., putting it in the hands of unelected technocrats with long terms of office and insulation from the hurly-burly of politics. The reasoning is the same as Ulysses': He knew he would get better long-run results by tying himself to the mast, even though he wouldn't always feel very good about it in the short run!

Although not entirely one-sided, most empirical evidence bears out this hypothesis, at least for industrial countries.[2] Researchers have measured central bank independence in a variety of creative ways, including a number of legal provisions, turnover of the central bank governor, the nature of the bank's mandate (e.g., is it directed to pursue price stability?), and answers to a questionnaire. A common, but not universal, finding is that countries with more independent central banks have enjoyed lower average inflation rates without suffering lower average growth rates, as depicted in figure 3.1.[3]

However, at least two qualifications need to be entered. First, the notably negative correlation between central bank independence and inflation that is apparent in figure 3.1 is not very robust. For example, it does not hold up when a larger sample of countries—including developing nations—is considered, nor when other variables are considered in a multivariate analysis.[4] Second, some recent studies have questioned whether correlation implies causation in this case.[5]

Having briefly presented the basic arguments for central bank independence, let me now raise a curmudgeonly

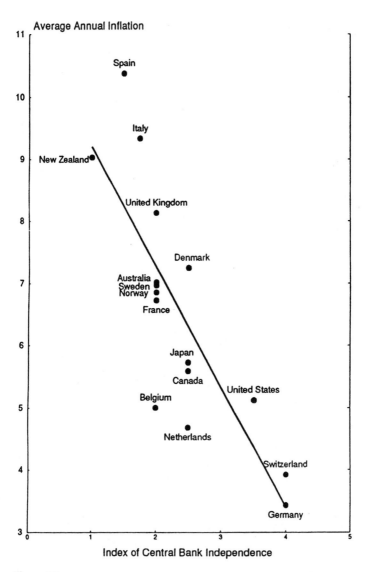

Figure 3.1
Central bank independence and average macroeconomic performance,
1961–1990

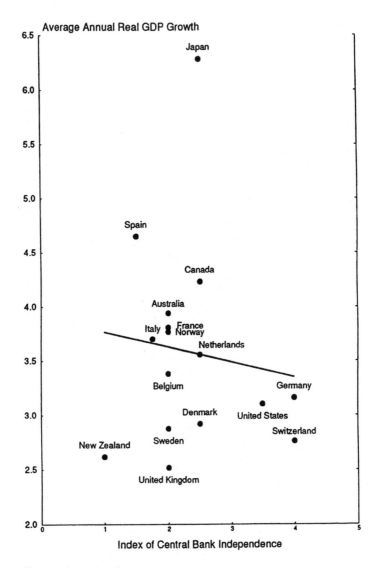

Figure 3.1 *(continued)*

thought. When you think deeply about the reasons for re-
moving monetary policy decisions from the "political
thicket," you realize that the reasons apply just as well to
many other aspects of economic policy—and, indeed, to
noneconomic policy as well. Consider tax policy as an example.

Decisions on the structure of the tax code clearly require
a long time horizon, just as monetary policy decisions do,
because their allocative and distributional effects will rever-
berate for years to come. There is a constant temptation—
which needs to be resisted—to reach for short-term gains
that can have negative long-run consequences. Capital levies
are a particularly clear example. Tax design and incidence
theory are complex matters, requiring considerable technical
expertise, just as monetary policy is. And decisions on tax
policy are probably even more susceptible to interest-group
politics than decisions on monetary policy.

Yet, while many democratic societies have independent
central banks, every one leaves tax policy in the hands of
elected politicians. In fact, no one even talks about turning
over tax policy to an independent agency. Why? I leave this
question as food for thought, perhaps for another day.[6]

3 The Central Bank and the Markets

So far, I have spoken about independence from the rest of
the government and therefore, by inference, from both par-
tisan politics and public opinion. This sort of independence
seems to be what people have in mind when they talk about
independent central banks, and it is certainly the concept of
independence on which both the academic literature and the

Maastricht Treaty focus. To be independent, the central bank must have the freedom to do the politically unpopular thing. But there is another type of independence that, while just as important in my view, is rarely discussed: independence from the financial markets.

Now, in a literal sense, independence from the financial markets is both unattainable and undesirable. Monetary policy works *through* markets, so *perceptions* of likely market reactions must be relevant to policy formulation and *actual* market reactions must be relevant to the timing and magnitude of monetary policy effects. There is no escaping this. It's important and of consuming interest to practical central bankers.

When I speak of making the central bank "independent" of the markets, I mean something quite different. Central bankers are often tempted to "follow the markets," that is, to deliver the interest rate path that the markets have embedded in asset prices. Living in a central bank for a while taught me how such a temptation arises. Central bankers are only human; they want to earn high marks—from whomever is handing out the grades. While the only verdict that really matters is the verdict of history, it takes an amazingly strong constitution to wait that long. In stark contrast, the markets provide a kind of giant biofeedback machine that monitors and publicly evaluates the central bank's performance in real time. So central bankers naturally turn to the markets for instant evaluation—or, rather, they have that evaluation constantly thrown in their faces.

Following the markets may be a nice way to avoid unsettling financial surprises, which is a legitimate end in itself. But I fear it may produce rather poor monetary policy, for several reasons. One is that speculative markets tend to run in herds[7] and to overreact to almost everything.[8] Central bankers need to be more cautious and prudent. Another is that financial markets seem extremely susceptible to fads and speculative bubbles which sometimes stray far from fundamentals.[9] Central bankers must innoculate themselves against whimsy and keep their eyes on the fundamentals.

Finally, traders in financial markets—even those for long-term instruments—often behave as if they have ludicrously short time horizons, whereas maintaining a long time horizon is the essence of proper central banking. Here is a stunning quantitative example of what I mean. You can use the term structure of interest rates on U.S. Treasury debt to compute implied forward rates up to 30 years into the future. While I was at the Fed, I asked the staff to use daily data to compute the correlation between changes in the current one-year interest rate and changes in the implied one-year forward rate 29 years in the future. Using 1994 as an example, the answer was 0.54![10] Now, you have to be a pretty devout believer in efficient markets to claim that the daily flow of news really has that much durable significance. I find that proposition totally unbelievable. Rather, I think, traders dealing with 30-year bonds behave as if they were trading, say, a one-year instrument.[11]

Notice the irony here. Perhaps the principal reason why central banks are given independence from elected politicians is that the political process is apt to be too shortsighted. Knowing this, politicians willingly and wisely cede day-to-day authority over monetary policy to a group of independent central bankers who are told to keep inflation in check. But if the central bank strives too hard to please the markets, it is likely to tacitly adopt the markets' extremely short time horizons as its own. This can create a dangerous "dog chasing its tail" phenomenon wherein the market reacts, or rather overreacts, to perceptions about what the central bank *might* do, and the central bank looks to the markets for guidance about what it *should* do. In the economist's technical jargon, this may come perilously close to creating a difference equation with a unit root.[12]

Do not get me wrong. I do not believe that a central banker can afford to ignore markets. Nor should he want to, for markets convey indispensable information—including information about expected future monetary policy. During my time on the Federal Reserve Board, I was constantly looking at and appraising the information in stock, bond, foreign exchange, and other markets as a way of divining how the markets might respond to a change in Federal Reserve policy. My point is simply that delivering the policies that markets expect—or indeed demand—may lead to very poor policy.

This danger is greater now than ever, I believe, because the currently-prevailing view of financial markets among central bankers is one of deep respect. The broad, deep, fluid markets are seen as repositories of enormous power and wisdom. In my personal view, the power is beyond dispute, but the wisdom is somewhat suspect.

4 Central Bank Independence and Credibility

In discussing the arguments for central bank independence, I did not mention a rationale that is often offered by central bankers and academics alike: the notion that more independent central banks are more *credible* inflation fighters and, therefore, can disinflate at lower social cost. Indeed, extreme versions of the credibility hypothesis, which have appeared in the academic literature, claim that costless disinflation is possible if central bank policy is completely credible.[13] The reason is simple. The essence of an expectational Phillips curve is that inflation depends on expected (not lagged) inflation plus a function of unemployment plus other variables and random shocks:

$$\pi_t = \pi^e_t + f(u_t) + \ldots$$

If expectations are rational and the monetary authority has total credibility, the mere announcement of a disinflation campaign will make expected inflation fall abruptly, thereby bringing actual inflation down with no transitional unemployment cost.

Omitting the credibility hypothesis was not an oversight. Much fascinating theory to the contrary, I do not know a shred of evidence that supports it. It seems to be one of those hypotheses that sounds plausible but turns out on careful examination to be false—like the interest elasticity of saving. The available evidence does not suggest that more independent central banks are rewarded with more favorable short-run trade-offs.[14] Nor does the recent experience of OECD countries suggest that central banks that posted inflation targets were able to disinflate at lower cost than central banks without such targets.[15] Nonetheless, these claims continue to be made, illustrating once again the power of wishful thinking.

Whether or not it trims the costs of disinflation, I can tell you from personal experience that central bankers prize credibility, viewing it as a precious asset not to be

squandered. And I agree, but not because it makes disinflation easier. Then why? A central bank is invested with enormous power over the economy; and, if it is independent,
that power is virtually unchecked. This authority is a public
trust assigned to the bank by the body politic. In return, the
citizenry has a right to expect—no, to demand—that the
bank's actions match its words. To me, that is the hallmark
of credibility: matching deeds to words. In fact, my dictionary defines credibility as "the ability to have one's
statements accepted as factual or one's professed motives
accepted as the true ones."

But academic economists typically employ a different
definition. In a game-theoretic setting, credibility is iden-
tified with either dynamic consistency or incentive compatibility. The notion is that, if the central bank announces a
policy and private decisionmakers take actions predicated
on belief in that announcement, the central bank must either
be bound by rule to follow through on its promise or have
a pecuniary incentive to do so. If there is neither precommitment nor incentive, policy may be time inconsistent and
policy pronouncements will therefore lack credibility. As I
noted in the previous lecture, this is the logic behind modern
arguments for rules that tie the central bank's hands or for
compensation schemes that give it a financial inducement
to behave. Each mechanism is viewed as a way to produce
credibility where it would otherwise be absent.

But when practical central bankers talk about credibility,
which they frequently do, they have a simpler definition in
mind—one closer to the dictionary definition. In their view
and mine, credibility means that your pronouncements are
believed—even though you are bound by no rule and may

even have a short-run incentive to renege. In the real world, such credibility is not normally created by incentive-compatible compensation schemes nor by rigid precommitment. Rather it is painstakingly built up by a history of matching deeds to words. A central bank that consistently does what it says will acquire credibility by this definition almost regardless of the institutional structure.

Thus, for example, the Bundesbank is believed when it declares its determination to reduce inflation, even though it follows no rule and its council members have no financial stake in disinflation. Furthermore, this concept of credibility is not a zero-one variable but a continuous variable; you can have more credibility or less. As I suggested in the second lecture, the Federal Reserve now probably has much more anti-inflation credibility than it had, say, in 1979. And it did not acquire this credibility through institutional change.

Here is an interesting question to ponder. The academic literature posits that central banks invest in credibility in order to improve the short-run trade-off. But there seems to be no such credibility bonus. Why, then, are central bankers so concerned with credibility? (Trust me, they are.)

Four answers suggest themselves, and I believe there is something to each. First, many central bankers probably believe the credibility hypothesis despite the evidence against it, just as many policymakers continue to believe that tax incentives will raise personal saving. Second, central bankers are only human; they want to be believed and trusted—not thought to be duplicitous liars.

Third, central bankers may want the latitude to change short-run tactics (e.g., abandon a money growth target) without being thought to have changed their long-run strategy (e.g., fighting inflation). To pull off such a feat without spooking the markets, it helps to have a reputation for keeping your word. An important example occurred in the United States in 1982 and 1983, when the Federal Reserve under Paul Volcker abandoned monetarism without creating fears that it was abandoning the fight against inflation. The Fed's hard-earned anti-inflation credibility helped make this transition successful. Similarly, the Bundesbank is constantly winking at its devotion to M3 growth; but few doubt its devotion to low inflation.[16]

Fourth, credibility can be a great asset during a financial crisis, when the central bank may be forced not only to take extraordinary measures, but also to *promise* to do so in the future as necessary. When a central bank's word is as important as its deed, it pays to be believed.

5 Central Bank Independence and Democracy

At this point, a deep philosophical question arises: Isn't there something profoundly undemocratic about making the central bank independent of political control? Doesn't assigning so much power to unelected technocrats contradict some fundamental tenets of democratic theory? My answer is: not necessarily. But I need to defend that answer in some detail. How can an independent central bank be rationalized within the context of democratic government? My answer is a blend of six ingredients.

First, we all know that, even in democracies, certain decisions are reserved to what is sometimes called the "constitutional stage" rather than left to the daily legislative struggle. These are basic decisions that we do not want to revisit often, and should therefore be hard to reverse. So, for example, amending the United States Constitution requires much more than majority votes of both houses of Congress. The founding fathers thereby made it almost, but not quite, impossible to change certain provisions of law.

Similarly with monetary policy. The Fed's independence—which derives from authority delegated by the Congress—makes it very difficult, but not quite impossible, for elected officials to overrule a monetary policy decision. Wise politicians made a once-and-for-all decision to limit their own power in this way just as, for example, the Constitution made it very difficult to change the length of the President's term of office. What made this decision "democratic" is that elected members of Congress made it of their own free will.

The second ingredient that helps make central bank independence consistent with democratic theory is something I emphasized earlier: The bank's basic goals are chosen by elected politicians, not by unelected technocrats. So, for example, when people suggested to me that the Fed should be content with 3% inflation, I answered that the Federal Reserve Act calls for "stable prices," not "pretty low inflation." If citizens think that's wrong, they should get the law changed.

Third, the public has a right to demand honesty from its central bankers—the point I just made in discussing credibility. The central bank owes this to the body politic in return for its broad grant of power. A central bank which dissembles or is imperiously silent is, in my view, behaving in a profoundly undemocratic manner. So are those who would cloak central bank actions in misleading rhetoric.

Fourth, the people at the top of the central bank should be politically appointed. When I went on the Federal Reserve Board in 1994, as a political appointee of President Clinton, I joined five other men and women who had been appointed by Presidents Reagan or Bush. None of us had ever been elected to anything; but Bill Clinton, George Bush, and Ronald Reagan had been. We obtained our political legitimacy from the men who appointed us; and they, in turn, got it the old-fashioned way: directly from the voters. That is as it should be. Central banks should not be self-perpetuating oligarchies.

The fifth ingredient, which I also mentioned earlier, should be present but rarely used: Central bank decisions should be reversible by the political authorities, but only under extreme circumstances. A Federal Reserve decision on monetary policy can in principle be overturned by an act of Congress. And Fed governors can be removed from office for cause. These mechanisms have never been used, but America is wise to have them in place. Delegated authority should be retrievable.

The final ingredient in my democratic stew is closely related to credibility, and I want to dwell on it at length. I will call it *accountability* and *openness*.

6 Central Bank Openness and Accountability

Because monetary policy actions have profound effects on the lives of ordinary people, a central bank in a democracy owes these folks an explanation of what it is doing, why, and what it expects to accomplish. As I often said while I was on the Fed, it's their economy, not ours. By offering a reasonably full and coherent explanation of its actions, the bank can remove much of the mystery that surrounds monetary policy, enable interested parties to appraise its decisions contemporaneously, and then—importantly—allow outsiders to judge its success or failure after the fact.

Greater openness is not a popular cause in central banking circles, where mystery is sometimes argued to be essential to effective monetary policy. Making the central bank more open and accountable, it is alleged, may subject it to unwelcome scrutiny that could threaten its independence. As Karl Brunner put it:

Central Banking [has been] traditionally surrounded by a peculiar and protective political mystique. . . . The possession of wisdom, perception and relevant knowledge is naturally attributed to the management of Central Banks. . . . The relevant knowledge seems automatically obtained with the appointment and could only be manifested to holders of the appropriate position. The mystique thrives on a pervasive impression that Central Banking is an esoteric art. Access to this art and its proper execution is confined to the initiated elite. The esoteric nature of the art is moreover revealed by an inherent impossibility to articulate its insights in explicit and intelligible words and sentences.[17]

I share Brunner's skepticism and could not disagree more with the argument that central banking should be opaque. In fact, I think it gets things exactly backward. To me, public accountability is a moral corollary of central bank independence. In a democractic society, the central bank's freedom to act implies an *obligation* to explain itself to the public. Thus independence and accountability are symbiotic, not in conflict.[18] The latter legitimizes the former within a democratic political structure. While central bankers are not in the public relations business, public education ought to be part of their brief.

Nor, by the way, do I accept the claim that more openness and accountability will harm the central bank—as long as it is independent. If the central bank makes good decisions, it should have no trouble explaining and defending them in public. If it cannot articulate a coherent rationale for its actions, perhaps its decisions are not as good as it thinks. Remember—and this is critical—I am talking only about explaining the decisions, not putting them to a vote!

In fact, I would go even further and argue that greater openness might actually improve the efficiency of monetary policy as a macroeconomic stabilizer.[19] Since this is an unconventional thought, I should explain why. In doing so, I will return to a point that I raised, but then dropped, in the previous lecture: that short-term interest rates differ from long-term interest rates.

Central banks generally control only the overnight interbank rate, an interest rate that is relevant to virtually no economically interesting transactions. Monetary policy has important macroeconomic effects only to the extent that it moves financial market prices that really matter—like long-term interest rates, stock market values, and exchange rates. I shall refer to these prices as "long rates," both as shorthand and because this is the price on which I wish to focus.

The standard theory of the term structure of interest rates is supposed to rescue the central bank from this dilemma. It holds that any long rate is the appropriate weighted average of expected future short rates, plus a term premium. So, for example, the one-year rate should reflect an average of the next 365 expected overnight rates—each of which will be determined by the central bank. Thus *expectations* about *future* central bank behavior provide the essential link between short rates and long rates.

Unfortunately, there are two severe practical problems with this theory. First, the expectations theory of the term structure turns in a very poor statistical performance. Statistical tests assuming rational expectations, for example, routinely reject the theory.[20] This result means that the forward rates implicit in long-term interest rates are remarkably poor forecasts of future short rates. Both academic researchers and market participants are aware of this finding and agree about it. Yet, curiously, economists, traders, central bankers, and the financial press all routinely use the yield curve to "read off" the expected future short rates that are allegedly "priced in" to long rates. It's as if all parties had somehow agreed to participate in a kind of mass delusion. I must confess to having done it myself!

The second severe practical problem with the expectations theory may explain its empirical failure and is crucial to my argument for greater openness. If the gear linking the overnight bank rate to long-term interest rates keeps slipping, the central bank will find it hard to predict the effects of its own actions on the economy. But the reaction of long rates to short rates depends critically on expectations of future short rates, which are, in turn, heavily influenced by *perceptions* of what the central bank is up to. A central bank which is inscrutable gives the markets little or no way to ground these perceptions in any underlying reality—thereby opening the door to expectational bubbles that can make the effects of its policies hard to predict.

A more open central bank, by contrast, naturally conditions expectations by providing the markets with more information about its own view of the fundamental factors guiding monetary policy. This conditioning ought to make market reactions to monetary policy changes somewhat more predictable, thereby creating a virtuous circle. By making itself more predictable to the markets, the central bank makes market reactions to monetary policy more predictable to itself. And that makes it possible to do a better job of managing the economy.

Please do not overinterpret this statement; I am no pollyanna on this score. Markets have minds of their own and often move dramatically for reasons that have nothing to do with monetary policy. There were speculative bubbles long before there were central banks to speculate about. So I neither claim nor believe that keeping the markets better informed about monetary policy will render them either stable or predictable. But I do believe that central bankers can reduce at least one source of speculative bubbles: bad guesses about their own behavior.

Here are two clear examples from recent U.S. history. I was not at the Federal Reserve in late 1993 and early 1994, just before it started tightening monetary policy. But I am fairly certain that the Fed's own expectations of future Federal funds rates were well above those presumably embedded in the term structure at the time, which seemed stuck at the unsustainably low level of 3%. A year later, I was at the Fed and I am certain that the market's expectations of how high the funds rate was likely to go—to as high as 8% according to various asset prices and Wall Street predictions—were well above my own.[21] In both cases, the markets got it wrong—once on the high side and once on the low side. In both cases, the faulty estimate was largely attributable to misapprehensions about the Fed's intentions.

And in both cases, the bond market swung wildly when it corrected.

Such misapprehensions can never be eliminated, but they can be reduced by a central bank that offers markets a clearer vision of its goals, its "model" of the economy, and its general strategy. Doing so would help anchor expectations better in some underlying reality.

The Federal Reserve, tight-lipped as it is, is far from the worst offender in this regard. In fact, it is probably more open and accountable than most central banks. But the competition in this league is not stiff, and I believe the Fed could and should go much further. For example, when the Reserve Bank of Australia changes short-term interest rates, the governor issues a lengthy statement explaining in detail the reasoning behind the decision and what the bank hopes to achieve by it.[22] These statements are actually meant to enlighten, not to confuse. They could serve as a model for other central banks.

Apart from this educational role, a second aspect, or perhaps definition, of accountability is related to something I dealt with in the previous lecture: rewards and punishments. In business organizations, the concept of accountability often entails bonuses for success and punishments for failure. Such incentives make people personally responsible for their actions and help align the employee's interests with those of the firm. This type of accountability takes a rather different form in central banking. Unless the central bank is a superb obfuscator, people will know that it is largely responsible for macroeconomic management. It will therefore automatically get credit (grudgingly, of course!) when things go well and blame when things turn sour. So, for example, the central bank governor may be rewarded with kudos and reappointment for success and punished with scorn and dismissal for failure. That's pretty fair accountability, it seems to me.

Finally, we can interpret accountability in the quite literal sense of accounting for your actions. In the monetary policy context, this means, e.g., periodic reporting of monetary policy actions and their consequences to the legislature, press, and public. Central banks vary a great deal in how much of this they do. At one end of the spectrum, there may be little beyond a formal annual report with no public questioning. Such a document is almost bound to be self-serving, much like a corporation's annual report. At the other end, we can imagine a central bank governor who is constantly subjected to public questioning by the legislature—which strikes me as altogether too much hectoring.

The Federal Reserve is somewhere in the middle of this spectrum, but probably more open than most. Since early 1994 the FOMC has announced its monetary policy decisions immediately, abandoning a long and deeply-held tradition of letting the market guess what it was up to. This small step, by the way, was once controversial and viewed as potentially dangerous. For example, Chairman Alan Greenspan told Congress in 1989 that a requirement for immediate disclosure of FOMC decisions "would be regretable [*sic*]". He claimed that "it would be ill-advised and perhaps virtually impossible to announce short-run targets for reserves or interest rates when markets were in flux," and that even in normal times "a public announcement requirement also could impede timely and appropriate adjustments to policy."[23] Now, however, the Fed's immediate-disclosure policy is universally acclaimed.

However, the Fed still offers very scanty explanations of FOMC decisions, fearing that its announcements would be misinterpreted, that ill-chosen words might lock it into future actions, or that changing circumstances might force it to change its mind—thereby undermining the doctrine of central bank infallibility. Before I served on the Federal Reserve Board, I believed the Fed could and should offer much more by way of explanation. Now, having been there, I feel absolutely certain.[24]

7 Conclusion

I conclude that central bank independence is a fine institution that ought to be preserved where it exists and emulated where it does not. However, as the lawyers say, it needs to be "perfected."

One important improvement would be to make the central bank's thinking on monetary policy more transparent. I have argued that such an innovation could both improve the quality of stabilization policy and make independent central banking more consistent with democracy. The arguments on the other side strike me as thin gruel. While anything can be rationalized by *some* theory, economists do not normally claim that markets function better when they are less informed.

I have also argued that modern central banks ought to assert their independence from the financial markets just as vigorously as they assert their independence from politics.

The U.S. Congress, for example, did not delegate the authority "to coin money [and] regulate the value thereof"[25] to the bond market; it delegated it to independent technocrats at the Federal Reserve. Following the markets too closely, I argued, may lead the central bank to inherit precisely the short time horizon that central bank independence is meant to prevent. There is no more reason for central bankers to take their marching orders from bond traders than to take their orders from politicians.

Notes

Chapter 1

1. One example is a central bank that must fix the exchange rate. A number of people have suggested that central banks should pursue price stability to the exclusion of all other objectives.

2. In the engineering literature on control of nonlinear systems in which the model is only an approximation to reality, smoothing of control instruments is often recommended because sudden, large reversals of instrument settings may set off unstable oscillations. A related problem in the economics literature is instrument instability (Holbrook 1972).

3. See Lucas (1976). While the Lucas critique has generated a huge amount of academic interest, it seems hardly to concern practical central bankers. Perhaps this is because they do not believe in regime changes. Or perhaps it is because they do not believe in econometric models. Probably both.

4. In Knight's (1921) terminology, these methods apply to cases of "risk" rather than "uncertainty." Risk arises when a random variable has a known probability distribution; uncertainty arises when the distribution is unknown. In the real world we are normally dealing with uncertainty rather than risk. And here, almost by definition, formal modeling gives us little guidance.

5. I should clarify what I mean. Used mechanically, the large models are not very good at forecasting "headline" variables like GDP and inflation—which is why virtually no model proprietors use them this way. But econometric models are an essential tool in enforcing the consistency you need to forecast the hundreds of variables in a typical macro model.

6. This statement seems to be a straightforward application of Samuelson's (1970) analogous proposition in the context of portfolio theory.

7. One very important condition is that covariances are small enough to be ignored. With sizable covariances, anything goes.

8. In the case of monetary policy, defining "no change" ($x = 0$) is actually a nontrivial problem. I will discuss where to locate the "zero" point on the monetary-policy scale in the next lecture.

9. With many random variables and nonzero covariances, the mathematics does not "prove" that conservatism is optimal. In some cases, parameter uncertainty will actually produce greater activism.

10. One strand, derived from the optimal control literature, deals with choosing among rival models. Another strand, due to Hendry and his collaborators, focuses on encompassing tests. See, for example, Hendry and Mizon (1993).

11. True optimal information processing would require weighting by a variance-covariance matrix.

12. Kydland and Prescott (1977) showed that it is an error to pursue dynamic programming mechanically if private agents base decisions on expectations about future policy. In that case, expectational reactions to policy must be taken into account. I take up Kydland and Prescott's critique in the next lecture; here I use the term "dynamic programming" generically, intending to include such reactions of expectations.

13. Beginning in June 1997, the Reserve Bank of New Zealand began publishing a three-year projection for monetary policy, stating clearly that only the next quarter's monetary policy is "desired"—the others are merely "projected" and subject to change. This closely approximates the dynamic programming approach. I am extremely grateful to the Bank's Governor, Donald Brash, for calling this innovation to my attention.

14. See, for example, Meltzer (1991).

15. This strategy has a temporal aspect not found in Brainard's analysis, and hence may embody a leap of faith. But Aoki (1967) offered a dynamic generalization of Brainard's result. Nonetheless, Aoki's result, like Brainard's, is fragile and may not survive, e.g., nonnegligible covariances.

16. From testimony given to committees of both the House and Senate on February 22 and 23, 1995, printed in *Federal Reserve Bulletin*, April 1995, p. 348.

17. See Gordon (1997).

18. See Eisner (1996).

19. Curiously, there is no such tradition of consensus decisionmaking on the U.S. Supreme Court, where 5–4 votes occur about 20% of the time. But over the last 20 years there has been only one 7–5 vote and one 6–4 vote on the FOMC, and there have been only seven other votes with four dissents.

20. An interesting exception is Faust (1996).

Chapter 2

1. A few papers in this spirit are Tinsley and von zur Muehlen (1981), Brayton and Tinsley (1994), and Bryant, Hooper, and Mann (1993).

2. Covariances and slopes of the IS and LM curves also matter. I ignore them here.

3. These tests allow for time trends in velocity, that is, they do not assume proportionality between nominal GDP and money.

4. Statement to the Committee on Banking, Housing, and Urban Affairs, U.S. Senate, February 19, 1993, printed in the *Federal Reserve Bulletin*, April 23, 1993, p. 298.

5. Bernanke and Blinder (1992) argued several years ago that the Fed has long used the Federal funds rate as its policy instrument. Most research since then has confirmed this finding, though perhaps with some modifications. (See Bernanke and Mihov [1995].)

6. The basic idea, of course, dates back to Wicksell (1898).

7. Bomfim's (1997) series is nominal and ends in 1994:3. In computing the real rate, I used the four-quarter trailing rate of change of the deflator for personal consumption expenditures.

8. Testimony of Alan Greenspan to the Senate Banking Committee, February 26, 1997.

9. See, for example, Blinder (1987).

10. Of course, some might interpret the fact that central banks allowed these shocks to pass through into higher inflation as evidence for inflationary bias.

11. In the case of some European countries, it can be argued that the European Exchange Rate Mechanism (ERM) was such an institutional

change; it effectively tied the country's monetary policy to that of Germany. But, for example, the United Kingdom and Italy broke out of the ERM, but still brought inflation down.

12. To be clear, ku^* is the optimal unemployment rate *if there were no worry about inflation*. So it is reasonable to assume $k < 1$ in the loss function.

13. Actually, many people had proposed such a scheme before. Walsh and Persson and Tabellini proved its optimality in formal models.

14. This problem has also been pointed out by McCallum (1996).

15. This is a statement about the theory. The data on advanced countries suggest that more anti-inflation central banks do better than this. Blinder (1995), for example, found no correlation between an index of central bank independence and the variance of real GDP growth. See Eijffinger and De Haan (1996) for a comprehensive survey.

Chapter 3

1. Actually, there is a third goal: "moderate long-term interest rates." But most economists believe that comes for free if you succeed in achieving price stability.

2. An important historical qualification should be entered. This evidence comes exclusively from the postwar period, when the problem typically facing central bankers was reducing inflation. Should the main problem change to combatting *deflation*, as was the case in the 1930s and very recently in Japan, it is not clear that independent central bankers will perform as well.

3. See, for example, Alesina and Summers (1993), Cukierman et al. (1992), and Fischer (1994). See Eijffinger and De Haan (1996) for a comprehensive survey of the evidence.

4. See Fuhrer (1997).

5. See Posen (1993) and Campillo and Miron (1997).

6. I offer my own views on this and related issues in Blinder (1997).

7. For a theoretical explanation based on short-time horizons, see Froot, Scharfstein, and Stein (1992).

8. The literature on financial market overreaction, begun by Shiller (1979), is by now voluminous. For a survey, see Gilles and LeRoy (1991).

9. Regarding fads, see Shiller (1984). Regarding bubbles, see Flood and Garber (1980) and West (1987).

10. The correlation moves around quite a bit over time. It was generally lower in 1988–1993, but higher in 1979–1987.

11. Things were probably quite different in the placid 1950s and 1960s. Then, bond markets were rather sleepy places, so traders seeking excitement had to look elsewhere.

12. Bernanke and Woodford (1996) make a similar argument—that such behavior may create "sunspot equilibria" even under rational expectations.

13. See, for example, Taylor (1983) or Ball (1994).

14. See Fischer (1994), Posen (1995), and Fuhrer (1997).

15. This statement is based on staff work at the Federal Reserve Board and Debelle (1996).

16. See Clarida and Gertler (1997).

17. As quoted in Goodfriend (1986).

18. This seems also to be the view of economists at the Bank of England. See Briault, Haldane, and King (1996).

19. The Federal Reserve has argued the opposite. See Goodfriend (1986), who is skeptical of the Fed's argument.

20. For a recent discussion plus references to the evidence, see Campbell (1995).

21. In the event, the funds rate topped out at 6%.

22. These statements are printed in the *Reserve Bank of Australia Bulletin*; see, for example, the September 1994 issue, pp. 23–24.

23. Alan Greenspan, Testimony before the Subcommittee on Domestic Monetary Policy of the Committee on Banking, Finance and Urban Affairs, U.S. House of Representatives, October 25, 1989.

24. In the month or so preceding the Fed's interest rate increase on March 25, 1997—which came well after this manuscript was in draft, Chairman Greenspan not only hinted strongly that a rate hike was coming but was unusually clear about his reasoning. Financial market participants, the media, and politicians all saw this greater clarity and openness as a departure from traditional Fed practice. I saw it as a vast improvement.

25. The quotation comes from the U.S. Constitution, art. I, sec. 8.

References

Alesina, Alberto, and Lawrence H. Summers, "Central Bank Independence and Macroeconomic Performance: Some Comparative Evidence," *Journal of Money, Credit, and Banking* 25 (May 1993), pp. 151–162.

Aoki, Masanao, *Optimization of Stochastic Systems* (New York: Academic Press), 1967.

Ball, Laurence, "Credible Disinflation with Staggered Price-Setting," *American Economic Review* 85 (March 1994), pp. 282–289.

Barro, Robert J., "Reputation in a Model of Monetary Policy with Incomplete Information," *Journal of Monetary Economics* 17 (January 1986), pp. 3–20.

Barro, Robert J., and David Gordon, "A Positive Theory of Monetary Policy in a Natural Rate Model," *Journal of Political Economy* 91 (August 1983a), pp. 589–610.

Barro, Robert J., and David Gordon, "Rules, Discretion and Reputation in a Model of Monetary Policy," *Journal of Monetary Economics* 12 (July 1983b), pp. 101–121.

Bernanke, Ben S., and Alan S. Blinder, "The Federal Funds Rate and the Channels of Monetary Transmission," *American Economic Review* 82, no. 4, September 1992, pp. 901–921.

Bernanke, Ben S., and Ilian Mihov, "Measuring Monetary Policy," NBER Working Paper No. 5145, June 1995.

Bernanke, Ben S., and Michael O. Woodford, "Inflation Forecasts and Monetary Policy," Princeton University, September 1996, photocopy.

Blinder, Alan S., "The Rules-versus-Discretion Debate in the Light of Recent Experience," *Weltwirtschaftliches Archiv* 123 (1987), pp. 399–414.

Blinder, Alan S., "Central Bank Independence, Economic Welfare, and Democracy," remarks before the Ingvar Carlsson Seminar, Stockholm, photocopy, August 30, 1995.

Blinder, Alan S., "Is Government Too Political?", *Foreign Affairs*, Vol. 76, No. 6, 1997.

Bomfim, Antulio N., "The Equilibrium Fed Funds Rate and the Indicator Properties of Term-Structure Spreads," *Economic Inquiry*, 1997 (forthcoming).

Brainard, William, "Uncertainty and the Effectiveness of Policy," *American Economic Review* 57 (May 1967), pp. 411–425.

Brayton, Flint, and Peter Tinsley, "Effective Interest Rate Policies for Price Stability," Federal Reserve Board Working Paper, 1994.

Briault, Clive, Andrew Haldane, and Mervyn King, "Independence and Accountability," Bank of England Working Paper No. 49, April 1996.

Bryant, Ralph, Peter Hooper, and Catherine Mann, *Evaluating Policy Regimes* (Washington D.C.: Brookings Institution), 1993.

Campbell, John Y., "Some Lessons from the Yield Curve," *Journal of Economic Perspectives* 9 (Summer 1995), pp. 129–152.

Campillo, Marta, and Jeffrey A. Miron, "Why Does Inflation Differ across Countries?" in C. Romer and D. Romer (eds.), *Reducing Inflation: Motivation and Strategy* (Chicago: University of Chicago Press), 1997, pp. 335–357.

Chow, Gregory C., *Analysis and Control of Dynamic Economic Systems* (New York: Wiley), 1975.

Clarida, Richard, and Mark Gertler, "How the Bundesbank Conducts Monetary Policy," in C. Romer and D. Romer (eds.), *Reducing Inflation: Motivation and Strategy* (Chicago: University of Chicago Press), 1997, pp. 363–408.

Cukierman, Alex, Steven Webb, and Bilin Neyapit, "Measuring the Independence of Central Banks and Its Effect on Policy Outcomes," *The World Bank Economic Review* 6 (September 1992), pp. 353–398.

Debelle, Guy, "The End of Three Small Inflations: Australia, New Zealand, and Canada," *Canadian Public Policy* 22 (1996), pp. 56–78.

Eijffinger, Sylvester and Jacob De Haan, *The Political Economy of Central-Bank Independence*, Special Paper No. 19, International Finance Section, Princeton, May 1996.

Eisner, Robert, "A New View of the NAIRU," Northwestern University, Evanston, IL, May 22, 1996, photocopy.

Faust, Jon, "Whom Can We Trust to Run the Fed? Theoretical Support for the Founders' Views," *Journal of Monetary Economics* 37 (April 1996), pp. 267–283.

Fischer, Stanley, "Modern Central Banking," in F. Capie et al., *The Future of Central Banking,* Cambridge University Press, 1994.

Flood, Robert P., and Peter M. Garber, "Market Fundamentals versus Price-Level Bubbles: The First Tests," *Journal of Political Economy* 88 (August 1980) pp. 745–770.

Froot, Kenneth A., David S. Scharfstein, and Jeremy C. Stein, "Herd on the Street: Informational Inefficiencies in a Market with Short-Term Speculation," *Journal of Finance* 47 (September 1992), pp. 1461–1486.

Fuhrer, Jeffrey C., "Central Bank Independence and Inflation Targeting: Monetary Policy Paradigms for the Next Millenium?" *New England Economic Review,* January/February 1997, pp. 19–36.

Gilles, Christian, and Stephen F. LeRoy, "Econometric Aspects of the Variance-Bounds Tests: A Survey," *The Review of Financial Studies* 4 (1991), pp. 753–791.

Goodfriend, Marvin, "Monetary Mystique: Secrecy in Central Banking," *Journal of Monetary Economics* 17 (January 1986), pp. 63–92.

Gordon, Robert J., "The Time-Varying NAIRU and Its Implications for Economic Policy," *Journal of Economic Perspectives* 11 (Winter 1997), pp. 11–32.

Greenspan, Alan, Testimony before the Subcommittee on Domestic Monetary Policy of the Committee on Banking, Finance and Urban Affairs, U.S. House of Representatives, October 25, 1989.

Greenspan, Alan, Testimony before the Committee on Banking, Housing, and Urban Affairs, United States Senate, February 19, 1993, printed in *Federal Reserve Bulletin* (April 1993), pp. 292–302.

Greenspan, Alan, Testimony before the Committee on Banking, Housing, and Urban Affairs, United States Senate, February 22, 1995, printed in *Federal Reserve Bulletin* (April 1995), pp. 342–348.

Hendry, David, and Graham Mizon, "Evaluating Dynamic Econometric Models by Encompassing the VAR," in P. Phillips (ed.) *Models, Methods, and*

Applications of Econometrics: Essays in Honor of A.R. Bergstrom (Cambridge: Basil Blackwell), 1993, pp. 272–300.

Holbrook, Robert S., "Optimal Economic Policy and the Problem of Instrument Instability," *American Economic Review* 62 (March 1972), pp. 57–65.

Knight, Frank H., *Risk, Uncertainty and Profit* (Boston: Houghton Mifflin), 1921.

Kydland, Finn E., and Edward C. Prescott, "Rules Rather than Discretion: The Inconsistency of Optimal Plans," *Journal of Political Economy* 85 (June 1977), pp. 473–492.

Lohmann, Susanne, "The Optimal Commitment in Monetary Policy: Credibility versus Flexibility," *American Economic Review* 82 (March 1992), pp. 273–286.

Lucas, Robert E., Jr., "Econometric Policy Evaluation: A Critique," in K. Brunner and A. Meltzer (eds.), *The Phillips Curve and Labor Markets*, Carnegie-Rochester Series no. 1, supplement to the *Journal of Monetary Economics*, January 1976, pp. 19–46.

McCallum, Bennett T., "Crucial Issues Concerning Central Bank Independence," NBER Working Paper No. 5597, May 1996.

Meltzer, Allan H., "The Fed at Seventy-Five," in M. Belongia (ed.) *Monetary Policy on the 75th Anniversary of the Federal Reserve System* (Norwell, MA: Kluwer), 1991, pp. 3–65.

Persson, Torsten, and Guido Tabellini, "Designing Institutions for Monetary Stability," *Carnegie-Rochester Conference Series on Public Policy* 39 (December 1993), pp. 53–84.

Poole, William, "Optimal Choice of Monetary Policy Instruments in a Simple Stochastic Macro Model," *Quarterly Journal of Economics* 84 (May 1970), pp. 197–216.

Posen, Adam S., "Why Central Bank Independence Does Not Cause Low Inflation: There is No Institutional Fix for Politics," in R. O'Brien, ed., *Finance and the International Economy* (Oxford: Oxford University Press), 1993, pp. 40–65.

Posen, Adam S., "Central Bank Independence and Disinflationary Credibility: A Missing Link?" Federal Reserve Bank of New York, 1995, photocopy.

Reserve Bank of Australia, *Reserve Bank of Australia Bulletin* (September 1994), pp. 23–24.

Rogoff, Kenneth, "The Optimal Degree of Committment to an Intermediate Monetary Target," *Quarterly Journal of Economics* 100 (November 1985), pp. 1169–1190.

Samuelson, Paul A., "The Fundamental Approximation Theorem of Portfolio Analysis in Terms of Means, Variances and Higher Moments," *Review of Economic Studies* 37 (October 1970), pp. 537–542.

Sargent, Thomas, and Neil Wallace, "'Rational Expectations,' the Optimal Monetary Instrument and the Optimal Money Supply Rule," *Journal of Political Economy* 83 (April 1975), pp. 241–254.

Shiller, Robert J., "The Volatility of Long-Term Interest Rates and Expectations Models of the Term Structure," *Journal of Political Economy* 87 (December 1979), pp. 1190–1219.

Shiller, Robert J., "Stock Prices and Social Dynamics," *Brookings Papers on Economic Activity* (1984), pp. 457–498.

Taylor, John B., "Union Wage Settlements During a Disinflation," *American Economic Review* 73 (December 1983), pp. 981–993.

Theil, Henri, *Economic Forecasts and Policy,* 2nd edition, Vol. XV of Contributions to Economic Analysis (Amsterdam: North Holland), 1961.

Tinbergen, Jan, *On the Theory of Economic Policy,* 2nd edition, Vol. I of Contributions to Economic Analysis (Amsterdam: North Holland), 1952.

Tinsley, Peter, and Peter von zur Muehlen, "A Maximum Probability Approach to Short-Run Policy," *Journal of Econometrics* 15 (January 1981), pp. 31–48.

Walsh, Carl E., "Optimal Contracts for Central Bankers," *American Economic Review* 85 (March 1995), pp. 150–167.

West, Kenneth D., "A Specification Test for Speculative Bubbles," *Quarterly Journal of Economics* 102 (August 1987), pp. 553–580.

Wicksell, J. G. Knut, *Interest and Prices,* 1898: translated by R. F. Kahn, London: Macmillan, 1936.

Index